NEW SCANDINAVIAN GRAPHIC DESIGN

GINGKO PRESS

NEW SCANDINAVIAN GRAPHIC DESIGN

First Published in the USA by
Gingko Press by arrangement with
Sandu Publishing Co., Ltd.

Gingko Press, Inc.
1321 Fifth Street
Berkeley, CA 94710 USA
Tel: (510) 898 1195
Fax: (510) 898 1196
Email: books@gingkopress.com
www.gingkopress.com

ISBN 978-1-58423-705-1

Copyright © 2018 by Sandu Publishing
First published in 2018 by Sandu Publishing

Sponsored by Design 360°–
Concept & Design Magazine

Edited and produced by
Sandu Publishing Co., Ltd.

Publisher: Sandu Publishing Co., Ltd.
Chief Editor: Wang Shaoqiang
Executive Editors: Jessie Tan, Chen Yaqin
Copy Editor: Jason Buchholz
Design Director: Wang Shaoqiang
Designers: Chow Pakwah, Wu Yanting
Sales Managers: Niu Guanghui (China), Winnie Feng (International)

Front cover project by Larssen & Amaral.
Back cover projects by Bleed, Bond Creative Agency, Snask, and Werklig.
Cover Design: Chow Pakwah, Wu Yanting

info@sandupublishing.com
sales@sandupublishing.com
www.sandupublishing.com

Printed and bound in China

CONTENTS

PREFACE

On Scandinavian Design

Growing up in Norway in the 80s, there was not much talk of Scandinavian design. It was a time marked by the influence of the UK and US in everything from music, design, and lifestyle—things that were considered the good stuff, at least for a young kid. At that time, I was too young to be interested in Nordic traditions or its design in general. But in many ways, the artificial expression of the 80s did not correspond very well with everyday life in Scandinavia.

The Scandinavian lifestyle is about closeness with nature. Almost every Norwegian family either owns or has access to a cabin in the mountains or by the sea for spending their holidays. These are simple houses, often without the conveniences of modern life. They are sturdy, rough, and made with traditional methods and the smart utilization of available raw materials. They can withstand the cold and harsh weather. This design aesthetic is as far from the white leather sofas of the 80s as you can imagine.

Luckily, when we grow older our perceptions and tastes mature, and that maturity comes from the culture and environment around us.

While the modern Scandinavian design movement was active as early as the 1930s, it began to gain global recognition and popularity, especially during the 1950s and 60s, resulting in a stable and lasting presence in today's culture. But Scandinavian design existed long before this, and will continue to. It is part of the Nordic culture, intertwined with the idea of social democratic equality.

There is an essential moral dimension, which has to do with the political and civic climate rather than the physical one. Scandinavia has long been socially inclusive, liberal, and tolerant, which has led to the shared conviction that the role of design is for everyone, not to serve a privileged minority. As a consequence, simple, understated, well-made design has long outshined the brief popularity of status symbols or showy, flamboyant effects. And it is more about the beauty of the practical and functional than minimalism. When you strip unnecessary clutter from something to make it more useful in your daily life, elegance and minimalism become a byproduct of that process.

I believe Scandinavian design is an aesthetic that has matured. These are expressions that have had time to develop and grow in an environment that is unforgiving when it comes to unneeded clutter. The dark winter days and few hours of daylight encourage designers to create bright and functional experiences. These traditional principles are being used in the new Scandinavian design, with usability and simplicity as the focus and charitable aesthetics. And this is what we see in modern design all over the world—Apple, Google, and countless other businesses are practicing something close to the Scandinavian design ethos right now. People want the beauty of unobstructed functionality in their lives, the pure shapes of the material best for the task at hand, the humanity of a well-thought-out concept. When our experiences with our environments become more friendly and attractive, life improves.

This is what Scandinavian design is and will continue to be into the future, and what this book is about.

Svein Haakon Lia
Creative Director/Founding Partner at Bleed
www.bleed.com

"

People want the beauty of unobstructed functionality in their lives, the pure shapes of the material best for the task at hand, the humanity of a well-thought-out concept. When our experiences with our environments become more friendly and attractive, life improves. This is what Scandinavian design is and will continue to be into the future, and what this book is about.

"

BLEED

Bleed is restless, intuitive, and contemplative. They defiantly question convention and the very definition of design. They not only think but more importantly, they take action. With a mix of cultures and disciplines, they create strong and sustainable value through strategy and design. With their eyes firmly set on the horizon, Bleed continues to blur design, art, and technology to create compelling products, services, and experiences for their clients.

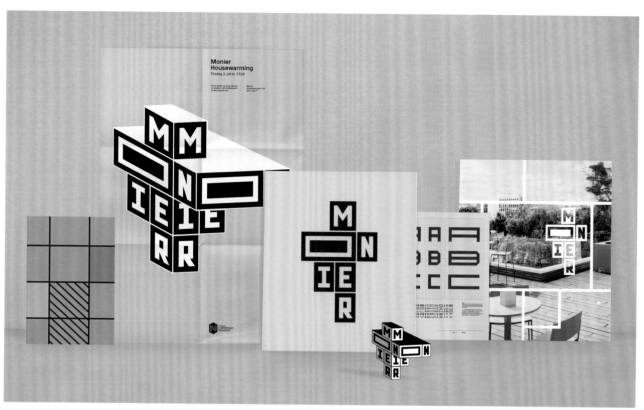

01. Monier Eng

Monier's visual identity is based on the building's architecture. The idea for the logo is derived from the building's three different window shapes, which are important characteristics of the building. As for the logotype, Bleed created a custom typeface where the alphabet is redrawn in three widths to fit within Monier's three window shapes.

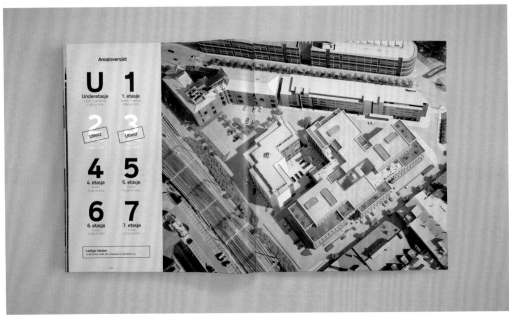

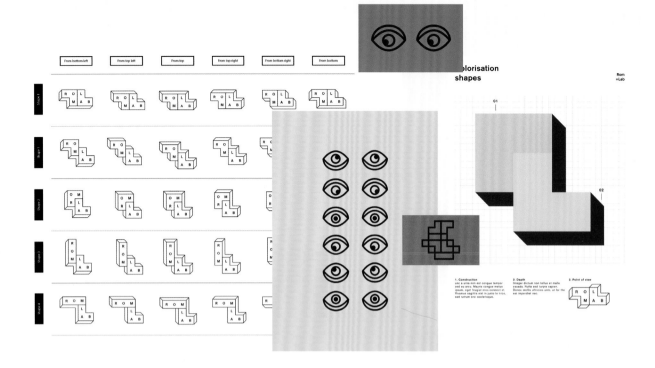

02. ROMLAB

This design identity comes from the name Romlab ("room" + "laboratory")
and resonates with the firm's philosophy of construction and experience
with space. Bleed kept the most intriguing and legible composition as a
logotype and used the other shapes as a foundation for the identity.

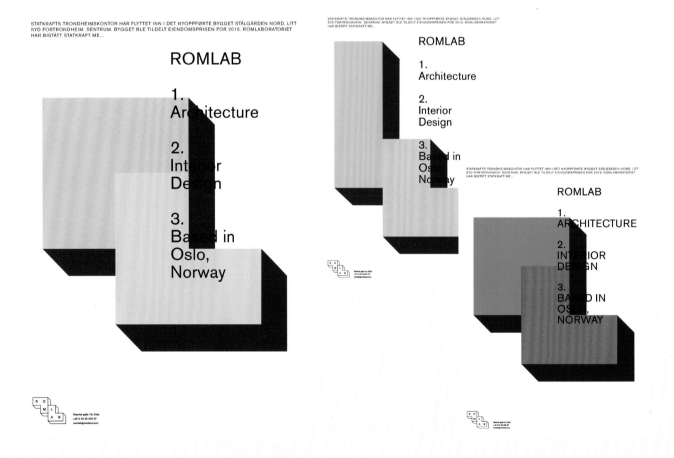

03. CLICHER

Clicher is a French company that prints photos and albums for young and creative people. Bleed created an application that generates infinite layouts of colorful shapes. In combination with the black and white logotype, the strict typography, and the compositions, the result is surprising and contemporary. The graphic system allows for different uses of shapes and makes the identity infinite.

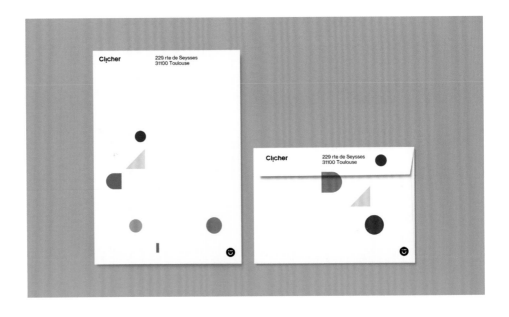

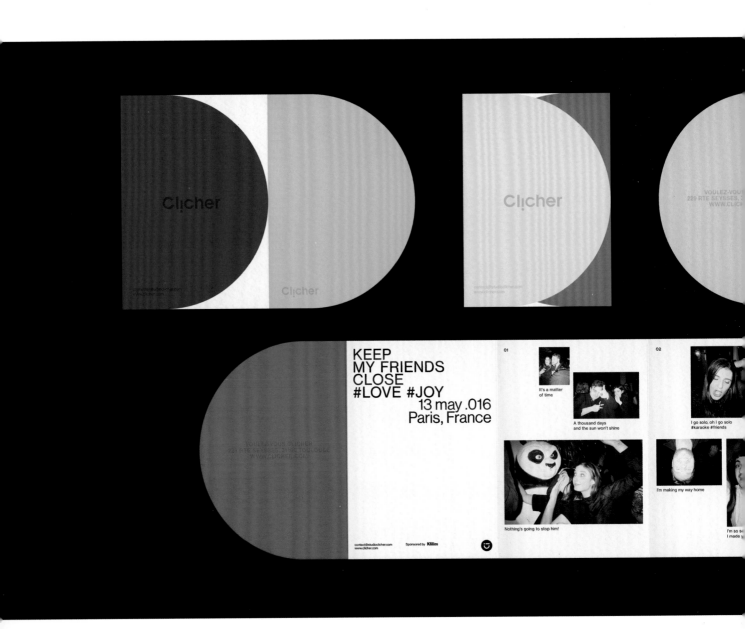

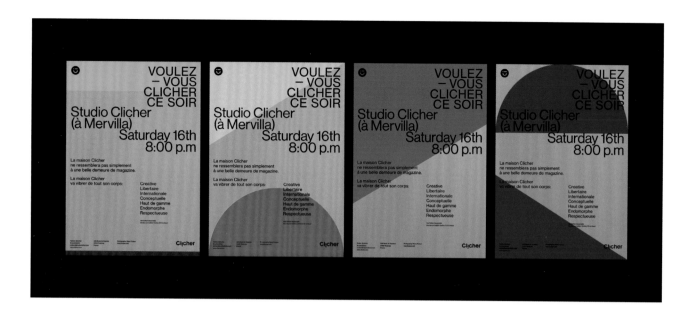

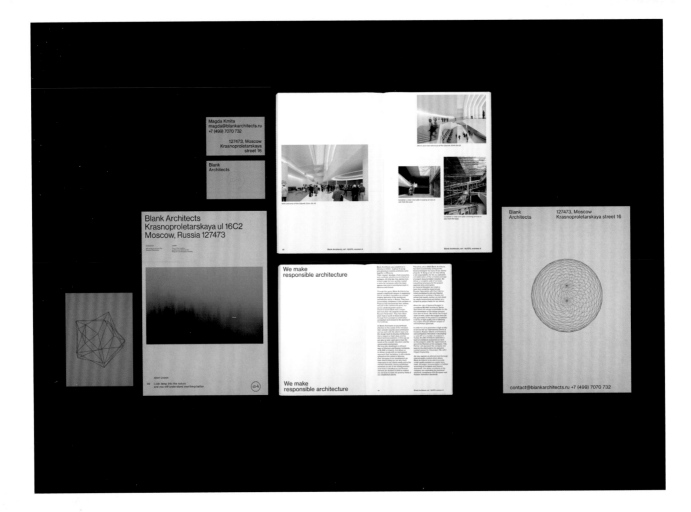

04. BLANK

Bleed started early in the process to think of ways to infuse code with design and to create visual links between modern architecture, experimental thought, and nature. The straight and uncompromising aesthetic of the logo and the stationery makes room for a series of code-generated pieces that can be implemented in conjunction with both web and print.

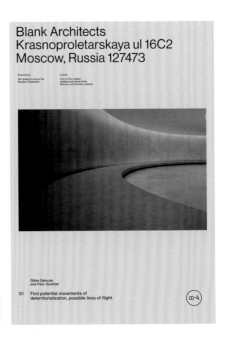

– 16.02.2016
Opening Theater London

Participants of World Architecture Festival including Magda Cichon (General Director of Blank Architects) told Archi.ru why it is interesting and important.
See directly Obratnyi otschot

– 01.02.2016
New Blank offices in Moscow

Blank Architects aim is to provide intelligent and coherent design. With a wide range of international partners we are able to provide our clients with all kinds of support in the following fields.

Latest Projects

Name	↓	Location	↓	Programm	↓	Status	↓	Scale	↓	Year	↓
Shopping center La Villette		Moscow, Russia		Landscape design		Concept		10 000-100 000sqm		2016	
Paleet Aquarelle		Paris, France		Commercial		Concept		95 000sqm		2014	
Mari, Shopping center		Paris, France		Commercial		Design development		150 000sqm		2017	
Fourniture Saint Pierre		Vienne, Autriche		Housing estate		Design development		409 000sqm		2015	
Paleet Aquarelle		Paris, France		Commercial		Concept		95 000sqm		2014	
Mari, Shopping center		Paris, France		Commercial		Concept		150 000sqm		2017	
Fourniture Saint Pierre		Vienne, Autriche		Housing estate		Built		409 000sqm		2015	
Shopping center La Villette		Moscow, Russia		Landscape design		Design development		10 000-100 000sqm		2016	
Paleet Aquarelle		Paris, France		Commercial		Concept		95 000sqm		2014	
Mari, Shopping center		Paris, France		Commercial		Concept		150 000sqm		2017	

Collection

Awarded
Shopping centers, Offices.

Shopping center Villette
(Moscow- Russia)

Nohamail
(Moscow- Russia)

Les Grands Homme
(Moscow- Russia)

No
(Mo

Collection

Cultural
Theaters, Cinema

Arena Park
(Moscow- Russia)

Arena Shopping center
(Moscow- Russia)

Shopping center Butovo
(Moscow- Russia)

Collection

Private
House, Office

Prvica Office Villette
(Moscow- Russia)

Paleet
(Oslo- Norway)

Office Dax Mimbaste
(Oslo- Norway)

• READ

05. Sbanken

The motivation for the rebranding and name change of Sbanken, formerly known as "Skandiabanken," was to pare away "Skandia," a step towards becoming an independent Norwegian bank. Through simplification, the new identity continues the bank's existing brand associations, further underlines the openness and simplicity, and stands out in a uniform industry. The circle represents the fact that Sbanken is there for its customers, regardless of where they are today, or where they are headed tomorrow.

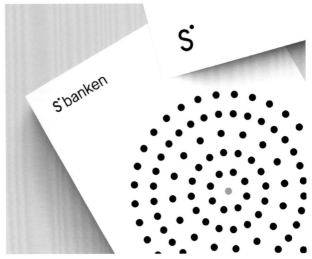

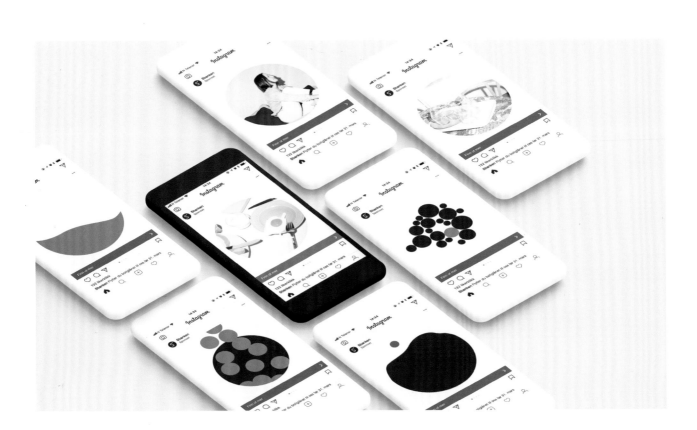

INTERVIEW WITH_
BLEED

Founder
Svein Haakon Lia
Dag Laska

Date of Founding
August 6th 2000

City, country
Oslo, Norway
Vienna, Austria

Founding Partner/Creative Director
Svein Haakon Lia
Dag Solhaug Laska

Partner/Creative Director
Kjell Reenskaug

Design Director/Head of Vienna office
Astrid Feldner

Project Manager
Marie Louise Notøy Steen
Camilla Dahl Torp

Senior Designer/Developer
Kristoffer Lundberg

Designer/Developer
Pedro Pereira

Senior Designer
Madeleine Eriksen

Designer
Camille Dorival
Bjørnar Pedersen
Listya Amelia
Marc Damm
Nicolas Vittori
William Stormdal

06. Tomwood

Tomwood is a Norwegian jewelry and clothing brand that embraces functional, timeless designs with attention to detail. Bleed designed a contemporary and effective identity that fits for both jewelry and clothes branding, where the logo is used mainly as a fine detail, atop a box or engraved on a ring, for example. The logotype has an international feel, making it easier for Tomwood to carry the brand globally.

YME
Karl Johansgate 39
0157 Oslo, Norway
THE LINE
76 Greene Street, 3rd Floor
New York, NY 10012, US

TOMWOOD
Prinsensgate 20

MONA JENSEN
FOUNDER & CREATIVE DIRECTOR

+47 975 80 390
MONA@TOMWOODPROJECT.COM

TOMWOOD
EST. 2013

OSLO NORWAY
TOMWOODPROJECT.COM

A/W COL. 2016

PARIS

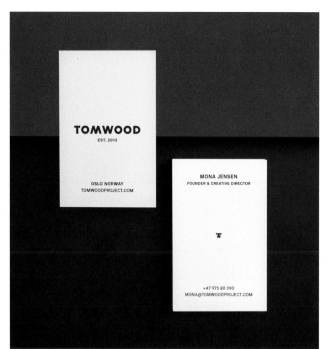

– 01. What drove you to establish Bleed? What is your vision for it?

When we started Bleed in 2000, it was just when the internet bubble burst. We all came from companies that had grown from five employees to infinity in a very short time. The culture was superficial and success was defined by growth instead of quality. We wanted to run a studio that created work we care about. We wanted to build a smaller but focused team who wanted to make change happen.

– 02. How would you define Scandinavian style? Does Scandinavia's design language shape who you are? In what aspects?

I think that the clarity and the "no bullshit" attitude of Norwegian culture are important to our work. Norwegians are not overly polite, nor into unnecessary pleasantries. We talk directly and this is also very much how we approach work.

– 03. How has Scandinavian design evolved over the years? How do you respond to the change?

I think Scandinavian design has become more self-aware and conscious of its own existence. In many ways, we are not very self-involved as a culture, so when we see and receive the world's attention and appreciation, we take it even further and purify it even more.

– 04. What role does Norwegian design play in Scandinavian design? Are there any lesser-known facts about Norwegian design you can share?

Norwegian graphic design is at a very high level. We see ourselves and other studios based in little Oslo as those

who really make their marks in the world. Also, Norwegian architecture and product design have really made strides in the past years. I think maybe Norway's role in Scandinavian modernism is a well-kept secret.

– 05. How do you stay innovative? How do you strike a balance between creativity and meeting your clients' needs?

There is seldom a conflict between the two. The concept is to do a job for the client, and we are always very focused on precisely what that task is. It is more important to debrief the client—not to take orders, but to strike up a conversation with the client about the real needs of a project.

– 06. You created a custom typeface for Eikund—can you tell us more about the creation of this typeface?

The Eikund typeface is grounded in a combination of Scandinavian modernism, the shapes of their products, and a vision of the new Scandinavian design. It has a subtle personality trait as do the company's products, which can be thought of as the vessel for the language they speak. Type design, like other designs, should be deeply rooted in a clear concept and meaningful functionality.

– 07. For you, what defines good design?

Meaningful change for the better.

– 08. What do you value most when picking your team members?

We always look for someone who is different from ourselves. We want our team members to have a different perspective and this is also very visible in our studio.

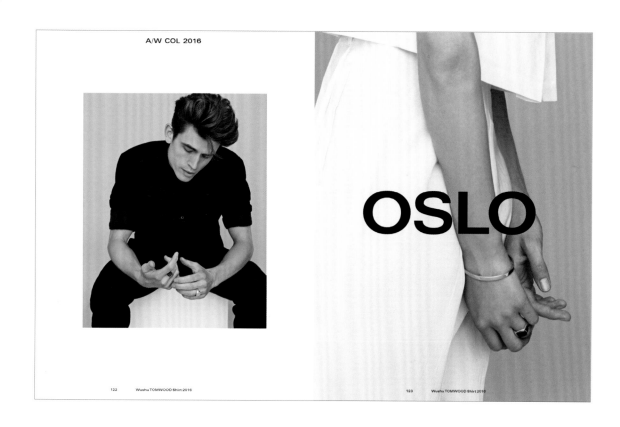

122   Wushu TOMWOOD Shirt 2016

OSLO

123   Wushu TOMWOOD Shirt 2016

TOMWOOD
EST. 2013

OSLO NORWAY

Morten

Hippe   coo

Øvre Hellelandsvelen 34,
4375 Hellvik
Norway

www.eikund.com
mh@eikund.com
+47 926 83 964

Eikund

segment. Bleed developed a
custom typeface by drawing
inspiration from the shapes of
the brand's furniture, making
it a natural extension of the
company's work.

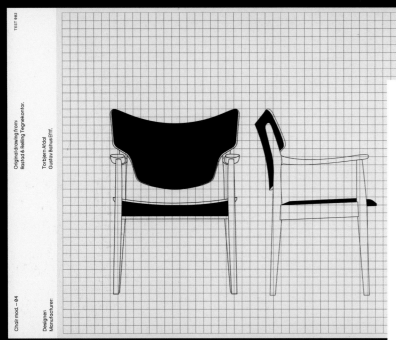

TEST #02

Original drawing from:
Rastad & Relling Tegnekontor.

Torbjørn Afdal.
Gustav Bahus Eff.

Chair mod. — 04

Designer:
Manufacturer:

Eikund Sans

Aa Bb Cc Dd Ee Ff Gg Hh Ii
Jj Kk Ll Mm Nn Oo Pp Qq Rr
Ss Tt Uu Vv Ww Xx Yy Zz &
00 01 02 03 04 05 06 07 08 09

Afdal   palisander
Bambi   Quart
Columbia   Røros
Danmark   Sauefell
Eik   Trevier
Faerøyene   Underlag
Gran   Variabel
Hollywood   Wegner
Island   Xavier
Jord   Yggdrasil
Kayser   Zoologi
Lenestol   Ægerøya
Mahogany   Øst
Nøytral   Årgang
Oker   Eikund

Oo

Aa

Kk

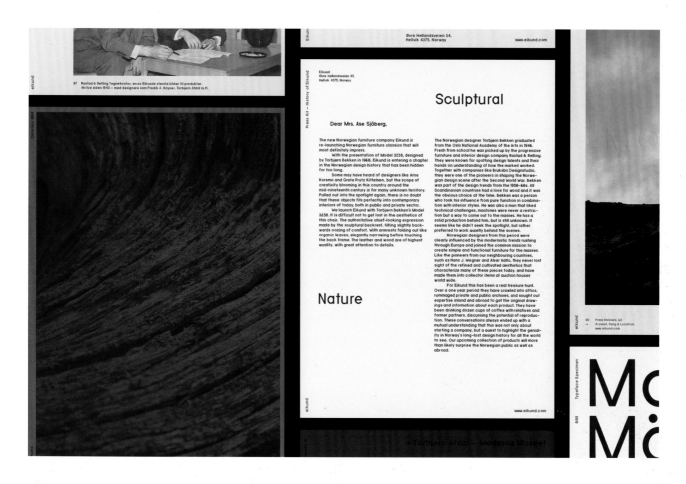

Meet

Eikund

About Eikund

The new Norwegian furniture company Eikund is re-launching Norwegian furniture classics that will most definitely impress.

With the presentation of Veng, designed by Torbjørn Bekken in 1960, Eikund is entering a chapter in the Norwegian design history that has been hidden for too long.

Some may have heard of designers like Arne Korsmo and Grete Prytz Kittelsen, but the scope of creativity blooming in this country around the mid-twentieth century is for many an unknown territory. Pulled out into the spotlight again, there is no doubt that these objects fit perfectly into contemporary interiors of today, both in public and private sector.

Contact
Sign up for Newsletter
Eikund on Instagram

The Norwegian designers from this period were clearly influenced by the modernistic trends rushing through Europe. Here shown: The Evja Dining Table

"The clarity and the no-bullshit attitude of Norwegian culture are important to our work. Norwegians are not overly polite, nor into unnecessary pleasantries. We talk directly and this is also very much how we approach work."

• • • • • Meet
¶
¶
Eikund

Afdal Bambi Columbia Danmark Eik Färøyene Gran
Hollywood Island Jord Kayser Lenestol Mahogny
Nøytral Oker Palisander Quart Røros Sauefell Treveler
Underlag Variabel Wegner Xavier Yggdrasil Zoologi
Ægeröya Øst Årgang 350 Characters.
Eikund Sans

OLSSØN BARBIERI

OlssønBarbieri has been working with packaging and brand identity since 2005. They are a design studio in pursuit of making changes. They do so by exploring the boundaries of both art and design to address the changing needs of consumers and to uncover new possibilities for brands to add meaning, purpose, and innovation beyond traditional marketing thinking.

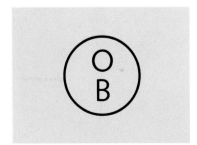

MODNET PÅ SHERRYFAT

HELLSTRØM
AQUAVIT

DESTILLERT, MODNET OG
TAPPET AV PUNTERVOLD
I GRIMSTAD

vare merke

KARVE...........................hele frø
SITRUS........................tørkede skall
STJERNEANIS..................frøkapsler
FENNIKEL.......................hele frø

NORSK AQUAVIT

01. Hellstrøm Aquavit

OlssønBarbieri reduced the choice of materials to the essential and selected only natural ones: the silkscreened glass bottle, the cork closure with an untreated wood top, and an uncoated paper seal. They wanted the bottle to communicate a premium and masculine look without compromising its functionality or ergonomics.

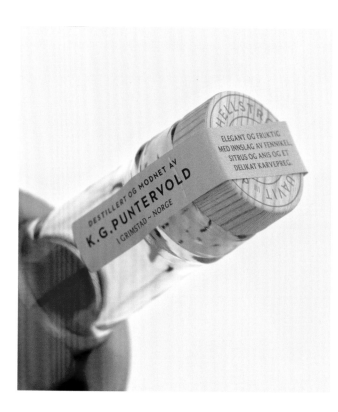

02. Snåsa

This custom-made bottle shape is both archetypal and timeless.
The colors and design elements emphasize an austere yet iconic
expression. Once the bottle is filled with water, the combination
of spray decor and silkscreen comes to life through refraction.

03. Balholm Fruitwine

OlssønBarbieri was asked by Balholm, a family-owned farm orchard, to create designs for a new range of ecologic fruit wines to tap into the renewed interest in old Nordic food and beverage traditions. By taking the language and typography of vintage fruit wrappers as inspiration, they created custom typography and illustrations for the brand. The bottles are wrapped in thin silk-screened paper.

04. Malbrum Parfums Vol.II

This packaging solution takes inspiration from vintage pharmacy packaging for the carton and adds a touch of craft and experimentation. The main label functions as a naming system and seal. Each bottle is sealed with a common self-adhesive strip. The boxes are foiled in black to create a memorable brand identity with integrity.

05. Balholm
Epledram 6666

Balholm Epledram 6666 celebrates the rich heritage and tradition of fruit growing in Norway. The tradition of micro-distillation is experiencing a revival in Norway thanks to a new law allowing for spirit distilling. To celebrate this renaissance, OlssønBarbieri wanted to keep the fruit at the center of the product to represent the country's orchards and farms, allowing for flexibility in naming and visual storytelling for future extensions in the product line.

INTERVIEW WITH_
OLSSØNBARBIERI

Founder
Henrik Olssøn
Erika Barbieri

Date of Founding
October 2005

City/Country
Oslo, Norway

Manager/Designer
Henrik Olssøn

Creative Director
Erika Barbieri

06. Gilde Juleaquavit

This project for Gilde Juleaquavit, a Norwegian seasonal Christmas Aquavit, was created to celebrate the 30th anniversary of the brand and the retirement of the master distiller, Halvor Heuch, known as the father of the Juleaquavit concept in Norway. The design for the jubileum, inspired by the tradition of giving flowers, commemorates Heuch's lifelong commitment and symbolizes festivity. The botanical designs include spices used in the distillation, as well as flowers and evergreens common during Christmas.

– 01. What drove you to establish OlssønBarbieri? What is your vision for it?

We met in 1999 in Italy while studying industrial and communication design at ISIA in Florence. After working together on some projects, we felt that we made each other work better. We eventually moved to Oslo in 2005 and decided to open up a studio together. Since then we have been driven to foster change. We do so by exploring the edges of art and design to address shifts in consumer sensibility and uncover new possibilities for brands to add meaning, purpose, and relevance that challenge the established truths. We love what we do and we welcome brands, collaborators, and people who think alike.

– 02. For you, what defines good design?

Good design can contribute to creating a better world through beauty, honesty, and responsibility.

– 03. How would you define Scandinavian style? Does Scandinavia's design language shape who you are? In what aspects?

Simplicity is a big mantra of the Scandinavian style. That said, our studio is half Norwegian and half Italian and through the years we have collaborated with talented people from Austria, England, Canada, Tasmania, and Portugal, just to mention some, so our style is definitely a result of cross-pollination.

Storytelling is a big part of our work and we employ our cultural heritage to build meaning and emotional connections.

– 04. How has Scandinavian design evolved over the years? How do you respond to the change?

Norway was under the kingdom of Sweden and Denmark until its independence in 1905. This may explain why Norway has been looking outwards for a sense of identity over the last 100 years or so. We think this is all changing now and

Norway is becoming an increasingly important contributor to the design scene across several disciplines, thanks to a lot of talented people working here. We like to think that our work is contributing to influencing this change.

– 05. What role does Norwegian design play in Scandinavian design? Are there any lesser-known facts about Norwegian design you can share?

We think Norway has finally found its own voice and its part of the conversation.

As a young nation, Norway has less heritage, which also means that it is a nation with a favorable climate for experimentation.

– 06. What is the most difficult part for you when you work on a new project? How would you solve it?

Every project asks for a different process. We believe research is essential to positioning and understanding a product and its context and eventually its potential in the market. In our process, we invite both cultural and historical aspects to inform and inspire us. The collection and analysis of these findings create the foundation and intuitively allow us to guide the concept development. We think the most difficult and exciting part is to trust the idea and work on it until it has reached its full potential.

– 07. How do you stay innovative? How do you strike a balance between creativity and meeting your clients' needs?

We are lucky that we are now attracting more brands and clients who put innovation as a key aspect of their brief. Innovation can, of course, mean many things. Sometimes it means challenging a category language while other times it means focusing on materials and production processes. We are always motivated to help visionary entrepreneurs to introduce a product that can challenge the market.

— 08. We see many packaging and branding projects for alcohol and wine in your portfolio. Is this out of personal preference or by coincidence?

When we started in 2005 we wanted to focus on packaging design. Wine was one the first categories we worked with. In retrospect, we see that back then wine labels were going through an important shift. Younger consumers did not care for traditional castles and since Norway does not have a long heritage connected to wine, the tolerance for experimentation was higher in this market compared to France or Italy, for instance. Spirits have also gone through a renaissance in the recent years with a growing number of independent and experimental distilleries, so now this

sector has become a strong area of interest for us. Today's industry is challenged category-by-category—niche perfume brands, the cosmetics industry, ecological food, etc.

— 09. Any upcoming projects or plans?

We are very excited about this year. We started working with a sustainable soap producer on structural packaging and identity, on a range of gluten-free products, on tonic water for an Indian client, and of course, some new spirits brands. We are also looking for a bigger studio. The future is busy.

07. Territoriet

This is a brand identity for the Oslo wine bar Territoriet, whose name emerges from its logo. The sound machine, inspired by futurist artist Luigi Russolo's *The Art of Noises* experiments, is a sculpture of the logo and an experimental music instrument that connects wine with music. Each bottle of wine has a unique card and plays a unique sound. High tones reflect young, light, and sparkling wines while deep tones a red wine with dark color, body, and aroma.

OLSSØNBARBIERI

"That said, our studio is half
Norwegian and half Italian and
through the years we have
collaborated with talented people
from Austria, England, Canada,
Tasmania, and Portugal, just
to mention some, so our style
is definitely a result of cross-
pollination."

BOND CREATIVE AGENCY

Bond Creative Agency helps new businesses and brands get started, and refreshes and revolutionizes existing ones for growth. Its services include identity, digital, retail and spatial, packaging, and product design. It brings together talents from different fields to create cross-disciplinary solutions for brands. Its team includes graphic, spatial, and strategic designers, producers, digital developers, copywriters, and artisans. Bond has studios in Helsinki, Abu Dhabi, and London.

01. WELL coffee

The core of WELL's identity is the wave-like element and the circular pattern, which work together to bring to mind a well and its waters, grabbing attention from pedestrians walking through the busy thoroughfare where the coffee shop is located. The water symbols were used in both printed materials and spatial designs.

WELL, HERE'S OUR MENU						
DEATH BEFORE DECAF			LATTE		4,50	5,50
DARK ROAST	2,70_		BUTTER COFFEE		3,50	
ESPRESSO	2,90	3,40	TEA		2,50	
AMERICANO	3,00		MATCHA LATTE		4,70_	
MACCHIATO	3,30		CHAI LATTE		4,70_	
CAPPUCCINO	3,70		CACAO		4,50	

02. Loupedeck

Loupedeck is a photo-editing console for Adobe Lightroom. Bond created the identity and website for the start-up to help build their business. The agile, communicative identity and web creation allowed Loupedeck to quickly launch their product to the market.

BOND CREATIVE AGENCY

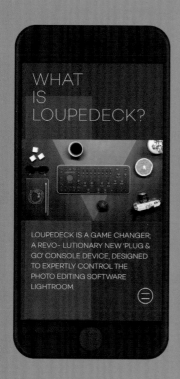

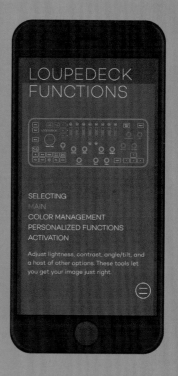

BOND CREATIVE AGENCY

Founder
Jesper Bange
Aleksi Hautamäki
Arttu Salovaara

Date of Founding
2009

City/Country
Helsinki, Finland
London, UK
Tallinn, Estonia
Dubai

Graphic Designer/Art Director
Jesper Bange
Marko Salonen

Retail and Spatial Designer
Aleksi Hautamäki

Strategic Designer
Arttu Salovaara

Creatives
20+ members

03. Paulig Kulma

Bond created a complete coffee customer experience for Paulig, which hosts a café, a coffee roastery, and a barista training program. The fresh and diverse urban place was designed for different customer groups and their needs throughout the day.

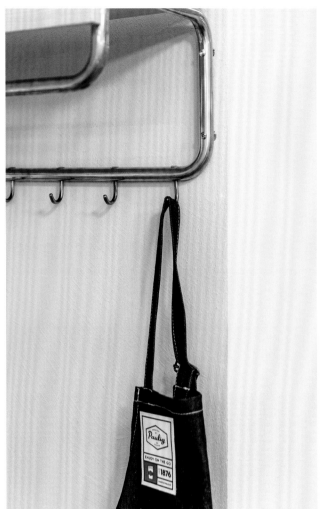

– 01. What drove you to establish Bond? What is your vision for it?

In 2009 the Finnish market was clearly in need of a new type of design agency. The agency market was going through a big change in the aftermath of the financial crisis. Bond was founded in Helsinki in 2009 by three people: Jesper Bange, Aleksi Hautamäki, and Arttu Salovaara, representing different areas of design. Bond is first and foremost an international and designer-driven agency, which centers on a design that stands the test of time.

– 02. For you, what defines good design?

Our design philosophy crystallizes to two words: simple, unexpected. These are the kind of designs we want to produce—simple designs that solve our clients' and the consumers' problems, and that are surprising, distinctive, and unexpected.

– 03. How would you define Scandinavian style? Does Scandinavia's design language shape who you are? In what aspects?

Nordic design is defined by minimalism and functionality. Our design has its roots in Nordic design, but we aim to add unexpected elements to our work. For us, Scandinavian design is a great tool and brand to communicate our agency internationally, because it is widely respected worldwide. Scandinavian design has become an internationally successful brand and approach that works all around the world, from Dubai to London and Seoul. At Bond, we make use of Scandinavian design's good reputation and use it as our starting point.

– 04. What role does Finnish design play in Scandinavian design? Are there any lesser-known facts about Finnish design you can share?

Finnish design brings the edge to the very minimalistic and mainstream approach of Scandinavian design. Finnish design is less polished. Scandinavian design overall has always been very democratic and non-elite, and in Finland, this is highlighted in a way where you can find designer brands such as Iittala in almost every home.

– 05. What is the most difficult part for you when you begin a new project? How do you solve it?

The challenge is finding the guiding idea for designing. The design should not just be a visual surface—the idea and the design thinking behind everything are what matters. We always aim to be creative with a purpose.

— 06. How do you stay innovative? How do you strike a balance between creativity and your clients' needs?

For us the important thing is bonding. This is actually where our name comes from—bonding with the client and close cooperation are the cornerstones of what we do. Ideas and creative directions are created through interaction with the client.

— 07. How do you determine the visual identity and put forward a scheme that works perfectly for a brand? Let's take Loupedeck as an example.

The starting point was to keep the Loupedeck identity at the core of the product. We wanted to keep the style modern, suitably technical, and minimalistic. We also wanted the identity to be a bit playful to highlight how fun and easy it is to use Loupedeck. It was also important to create a holistic brand, where the console, software, packaging, webshop, and marketing are one seamless experience.

— 08. What do you value most when picking your team members?

Of course, creative problem-solving is important, but the ability to take responsibility is also a trait we value highly. When looking for new people to join our team we are also looking for them to fit in with our bunch.

— 09. Any upcoming projects or plans?

We recently opened a new studio in Tallinn. We are also currently working on projects such as designing the new identity of Khalifa University in the UAE and a restaurant concept where the Asian flavors are the starting point.

04. Roster

Roster is a bar, restaurant, and a vibrant meeting place in the heart of Helsinki. Its design complements the style of the cuisine. The interiors are a mix of captivating elements: custom-made furniture with a vintage twist, both raw and refined materials, and handpicked design objects.

"Nordic design is defined by minimalism and functionality. Our design has its roots in Nordic design, but we aim to add unexpected elements to our work."

BOND CREATIVE AGENCY

LUNDGREN+
LINDQVIST

SWEDEN

- Graphic Design
- Art Direction
- Web Design

Lundgren+Lindqvist is a Sweden-based design studio led by founding partners Andreas Friberg Lundgren and Carl-Johan Lindqvist. With an approach that is conceptually driven, the studio has built an international reputation for crafting high-quality solutions that are equally compelling to the eyes and the intellect. Since its establishment in 2007, the studio has utilized code as a tool as natural to the design process as pen and paper. Although simple in form, the output is often multi-layered and built upon an in-depth understanding of the project's prerequisites.

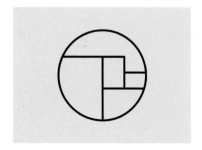

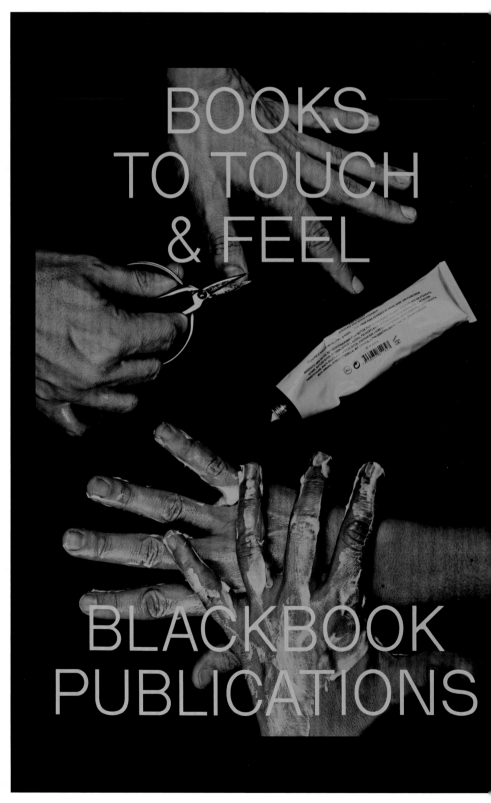

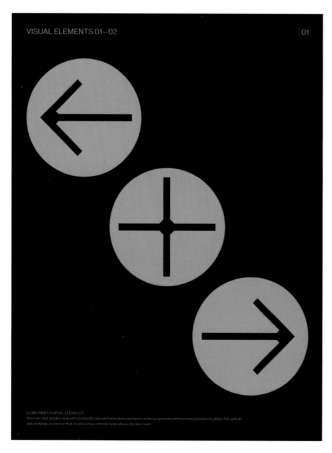

ICONS AND GRAPHIC ELEMENTS:
The icons and graphic elements used by Blackbook Publications are based on the proportions of the primary typeface (Lettera Txt), with an added ink trap in reverse that creates a characteristic lump where strockes meet.

Artists published to date: Simon Berg, Kalle Sanner, Agnes Thor, Emmanuel Cederqvist, Johan Markusson, Lotta Törnroth, Linda Hofvander, Signe Vad and Anais Boudot. Webshop - blackbookpublications.com

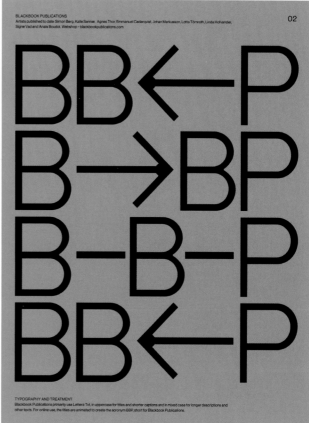

TYPOGRAPHY AND TREATMENT
Blackbook Publications primarily use Lettera Txt, in uppercase for titles and shorter captions and in mixed case for longer descriptions and other texts. For online use, the titles are animated to create the acronym BBP, short for Blackbook Publications.

01. Blackbook Publications

Lundgren+Lindqvist opted for integrating the profile text and contact information into the menu overlay of Blackbook's website, allowing visitors to quickly access information. The hands in the images emphasize that these are books that are meant to be touched and felt.

BOOKS TOUCH & FEEL BOOKS

TYPOGRAPHIC TREATMENT:

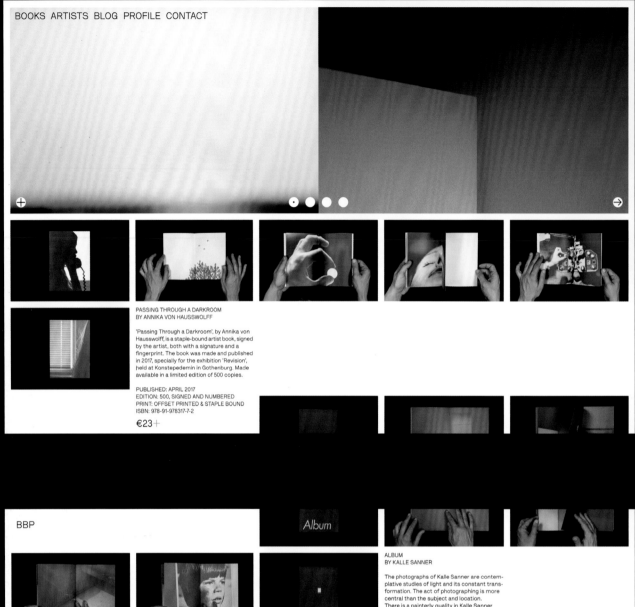

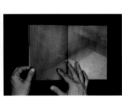   

PASSING THROUGH A DARKROOM
BY ANNIKA VON HAUSSWOLFF

'Passing Through a Darkroom', by Annika von
Hausswolff, is a staple-bound artist book, signed
by the artist, both with a signature and a
fingerprint. The book was made and published
in 2017, specially for the exhibition 'Revision',
held at Konstepedernin in Gothenburg. Made
available in a limited edition of 500 copies.

PUBLISHED: APRIL 2017
EDITION: 500, SIGNED AND NUMBERED
PRINT: OFFSET PRINTED & STAPLE BOUND
ISBN: 978-91-978317-7-2

€23 +

BBP

Album

ALBUM
BY KALLE SANNER

The photographs of Kalle Sanner are contemplative studies of light and its constant trans-
formation. The act of photographing is more
central than the subject and location.
There is a painterly quality in Kalle Sanner
photographs and the darkest ones recall Mark
Rothko's saturated and rust-red images. He
dwells not in the gloom but allows light to
guide him through the rooms... If photographs
are drawings in light you could say that Kalle
Sanner's portrait of light actually captures
the essence of photography."
– Excerpt from catalouge, Dragana Vujanovic,
Curator Hasselblad Foundation

PUBLISHED: 2010
EDITION: 300
PRINT: OFFSET PRINTED & STAPLE BOUND
ISBN: 978-91-978317-2-7

€18 +

BUTIKEN
BY JOHAN MARKUSSON

At first sight it might look rigid, but in the en-
counters between customers and employees,
there are humorous and poetic elements.
This fictive story takes place in a store where
the customers are being helped at the counter.
Employees organize goods for the customers,
utilitising carts and packing lists.

FORMAT: 135 × 220 MM
EDITION: 200
PUBLISHED: 2015
ISBN: 978-91-978317-7-2

€13 +

02. Ord-Bild Notebooks

During a visit to Lisbon, Lundgren+Lindqvist happened upon a
set of delicate, handmade notebooks from the brand Namban.
They co-designed a special edition of the notebooks for
Ll'Editions. The result is the Ord-Bild notebooks, released in
an edition of 25 sets—each containing two notebooks and a
hand-numbered brass token, housed in a staple-bound, flat-
foiled box.

03. Roger Burkhard

Roger Burkhard is a creative web development studio based in Switzerland. The new visual identity of the studio revolves around a modular system with a baseline grid constituting its smallest visual component. Lundgren+Lindqvist designed a monogram, featuring a reversed capital "R" for "Roger," conjoined with a capital "B" for "Burkhard." The monogram's thin lines are accentuated by a silver spot color on the dark gray paper used for the stationery.

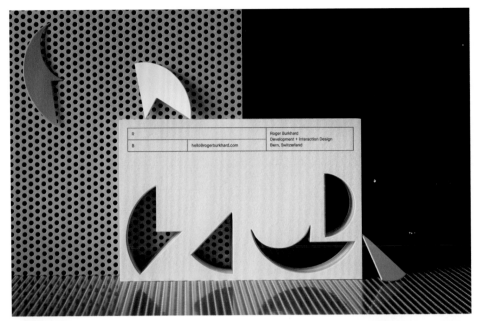

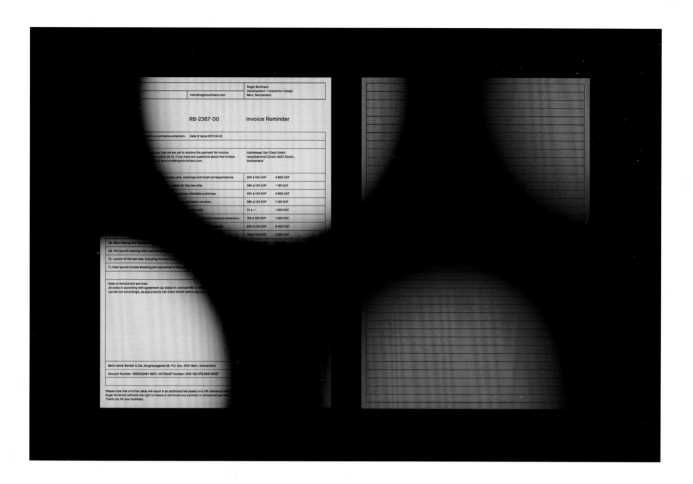

INTERVIEW WITH_
LUNDGREN+LINDQVIST

Founder
Andreas Friberg Lundgren
Carl-Johan Lindqvist

Date of Founding
2007

City/Country
Gothenburg, Sweden

Co-Founder/Art Director
Andreas Friberg Lundgren

Web Developer/Co-Founder
Carl-Johan Lindqvist

Graphic Designer
Julius Åsling

Web Developer
Fredrik Ekelund

Front-end Developer
Christian Jánský

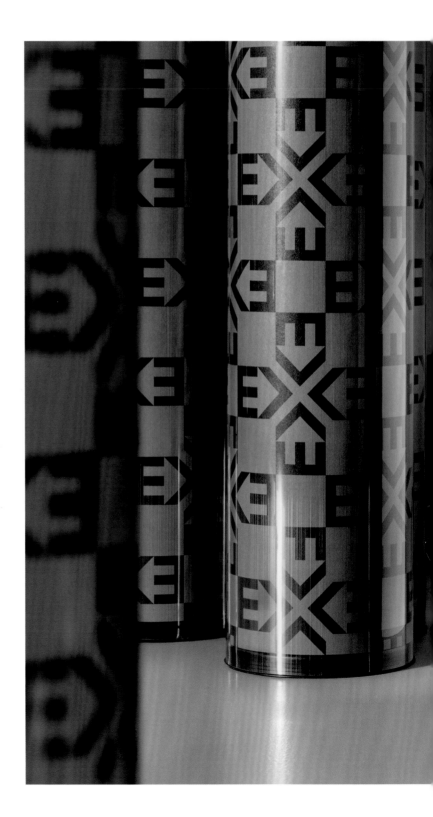

04. Enter Arkitektur

Enter Arkitektur is a Swedish architectural practice that was founded in the 1950s. For the renewal of the brand's identity, Lundgren+Lindqvist outlined two architectural typologies: a) history and heritage and b) contemporary architecture, which both bear equal importance to Enter. The result emerged as a new brandmark that combines a capital "E" for "Enter" with an arrowhead, which refers to the growth of Enter and its connection with clients. To unite these two elements, the designers also formed the first architectural typology in the resulting negative space and the second in the new mark's outline.

– 01. What drove you to establish Lundgren+Lindqvist? What is your vision for it?

Lundgren+Lindqvist was initially established through an organic process where two collaborating freelance businesses almost seamlessly merged into a joint venture. Over the years we have established a clearer vision which, while somewhat abstract, focuses mainly on working on projects for people we respect. We continually question where we are headed and how we are doing things in order to avoid stagnation and to keep things new and exciting.

– 02. For you, what defines good design?

Good design is the combination of a strong concept and flawless execution. Good design is honest and speaks to its intended audience in a language and tone that they both understand and feel comfortable with.

– 03. How would you define Scandinavian style? Does Scandinavia's design language shape who you are? In what aspects?

Seen from a historical perspective, the Scandinavian post-modernist design language deals with basics. Generally speaking, a limited color palette and limited use of ornamentation, with the occasional illustration, have been the common approach. In the fields of graphic design and advertising, Swedes have been very influenced by the approach and work of Doyle Dane Bernbach (DDB) in the late 1950's. The "Think Small" campaign for Volkswagen is a great example. This tradition was carried on in Sweden by legendary Swedish art directors and graphic designers like

John Melin & Anders Österlin (M&Ö) and Olle Eksell. As a Swede, it is also hard not to be affected, either consciously or sub-consciously, by the work of great architects like Gunnar Asplund, Sigurd Lewerentz, and Bruno Mathsson. In Denmark, you have Arne Jacobsen, Hans J Wegner, and Finn Juhl, and in Finland, the legacy of Alvar Aalto and the work of Yrjö Kukkapuro and Eero Saarinen, to mention but a few.

– 04. How has Scandinavian design evolved over the years? How do you respond to the change?

As a result of globalization, I think regional differences are becoming increasingly blurred. Whether you are from Sweden, Poland or Ghana, you more or less have access to the same sources of inspiration through computers, tablets, and phones. Our response to this does not have so much to do with nationality, as with an aim to have a voice of our own. By finding inspiration from the same sources as everybody else, we run the risk of drowning in a pool of sameness. Therefore, we are more likely to find inspiration in a book at an antiquarian rather than on Instagram. That being said, we do love Instagram and similar services for the quick access and updates they provide.

– 05. What is the most difficult part for you when you work on a new project? How do you solve it?

A crucial aspect is definitely to establish a strong relationship with our client. It is only by gaining their trust that we will be able to do something truly interesting. There is no fast lane to getting there, but being a good listener usually helps.

– 06. How do you stay innovative? How do you strike a balance between creativity and your clients' needs?

Luckily, many new clients approach us because they want something that responds to their brief, but also pushes the envelope in terms of creativity. By avoiding generalization and trusting in the recipients' (the client's clients) ability to appreciate and comprehend what we are trying to say, we are able to steer clear of the type of focus-group solutions that are shoved down your throat on a daily basis. Bad design is ever-so-often the result of believing in established formulas like girls preferring pink while boys like blue.

– 07. What is your design process? Let's take your project Roger Burkhard as an example.

When working on a project like the one for Roger Burkhard, we always start out by learning as much as possible about the client and their field of business. In the case of Roger Burkhard, being a web development studio, we of course already knew the field very well. After we have gotten to know the client and their work, we move on to a phase of abstract, conceptual work. In this phase, we establish the foundation for the actual design work that is to follow. In the design phase, we work on a number of rough executions of one or a few concepts, which we subsequently narrow down to one proposal—the one we present to our client. If this proposal is accepted, we then go on to fine-tune it before starting to design the various items outlined in the brief. If the initial proposal is rejected, we will revisit the earlier stages of the process and present a new solution to the client.

– 08. As a multi-disciplinary studio with services covering visual identity design, art direction, and design for print and web, what do you think are the things these disciplines have in common?

In our process, design is code and code is design. While some of our projects have digital components and others do not, we enjoy approaching the design of a publication as if it is a website and treat the design like we would do for a digital project. Apart from viewing these related disciplines as different tools in a toolbox, it is also a way of constantly avoiding a routine. A common trait amongst the people working for us is that they are curious individuals who thrive in an environment where they are constantly exposed to new challenges.

"Seen from a historical perspective, the Scandinavian post-modernist design language deals with basics. Generally speaking, a limited color palette and limited use of ornamentation, with the occasional illustration, have been the common approach."

05. MCKNGBRD

MCKNGBRD is a brand that makes premium cases for laptops and tablets. The brand name is both semantically and phonetically related to the name of the founder, "Mokhberi," and the word "mockingbird." By removing the vowels, Lundgren+Lindqvist created a shorter and more distinctly unique wordmark, prompting the reader to interact with the brand through filling the gaps in the familiar word.

OEDIPE

Oedipe is a Copenhagen-based design practice run by designer Peter Orban, specializing in creative direction and graphic design at the intersection of design and art. They work with clients from the fields of fashion, gastronomy, beauty, and lifestyle.

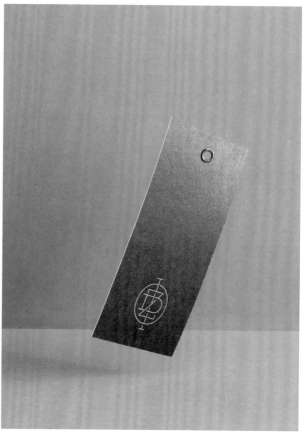

01. Division Ozwald

Division Ozwald's logo features the first letters of the brand name with an emphasis on aesthetic nuance. The identity appears in black and white tones yet a set of highly detailed material components are introduced to impart a deep and sophisticated voice.

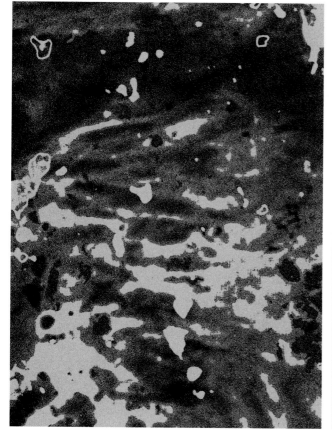

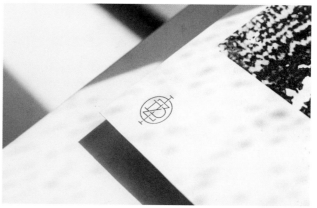

02. S'Oil

The identity of S'Oil consists of some carefully designed and selected elements: a series of monochrome illustrations in dark grey and pastel colors, a minimalist symbol, and a modernized coat of arms, tying the brand to its origins.

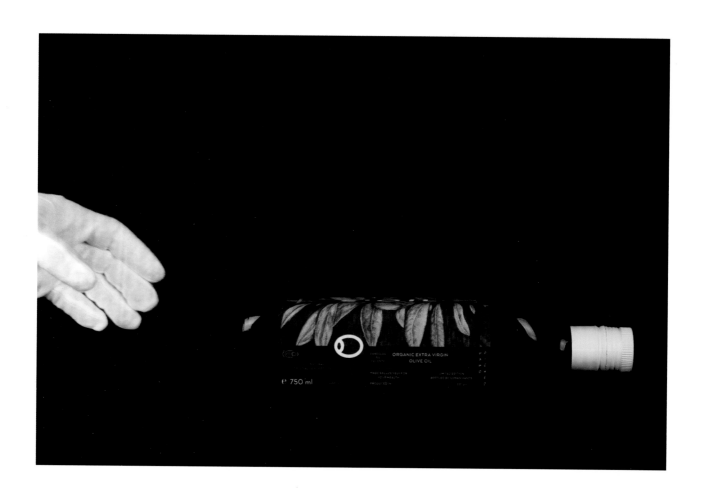

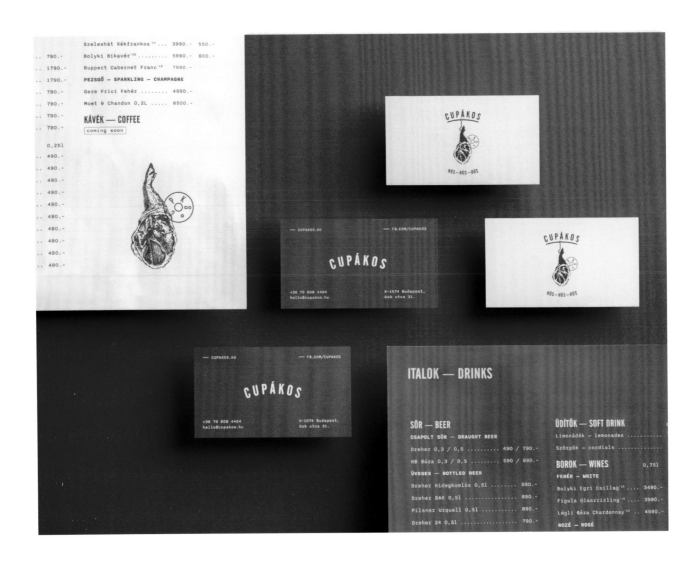

03. Cupákos
Restaurant

The visual identity is comprised of the combination of very simple elements such as hand-drawn illustrations, blue meat stamps, and a condensed typeface. The bar features an interior design that mixes bold red tones and brighter, natural elements.

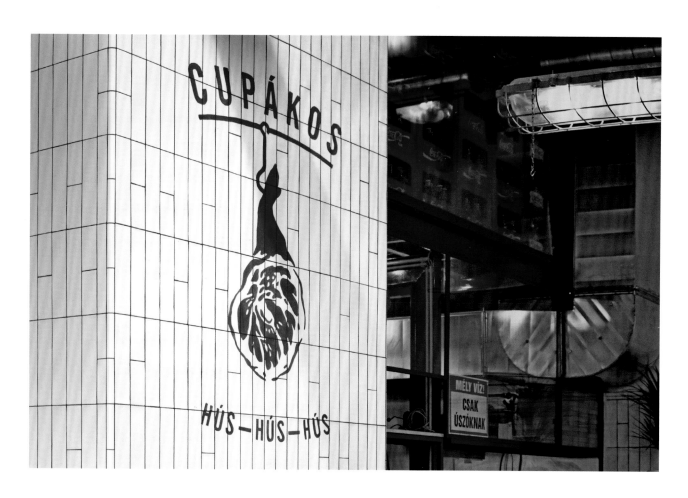

"We are born out of a desire to work more with fashion, art, design, and lifestyle brands."

SNASK

• Graphic Design
• Art Direction
• Branding

Snask strives to challenge the industry by doing things differently. They worship unconventional ideas, charming smiles, and real emotions. They see the old conservative world as extremely tedious and as their biggest enemy.

SNaSK

01. Wauw!

Snask chose a black case for Wauw! to differentiate the packaging from its ice cream competitors and used a "tasty" and "kind" typography and form to avoid the luxury bracket.

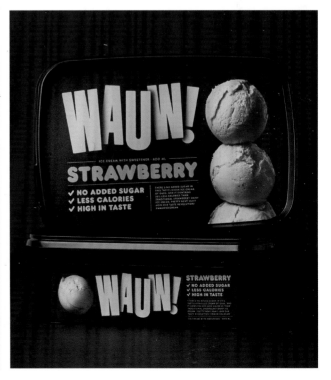

02. Shower Beer

Shower Beer is a sweet but strong pale ale, in a small bottle of 18cl. The lettering is screen-printed in pink on the brown glass bottle, giving the brand a slender, elegant, and distinctive look.

03. Froda

Snask gave this financial services brand a very down-to-earth tone of voice as well as a bold and colorful visual identity. They created Froda's identity by taking geometric and colorful pieces from different materials and assembling them into a complete design system that stretches from logotype to icons and patterns.

Få svar inom
24 timmar!

Fast pris utan
dolda avgifter!

04. Kaibosh

Snask translated this brand and tonality into visual form and matched it with a custom-made display typeface. The graphic elements of the eyelashes, a symbol to distinguish the identity, appear in many different scenarios.

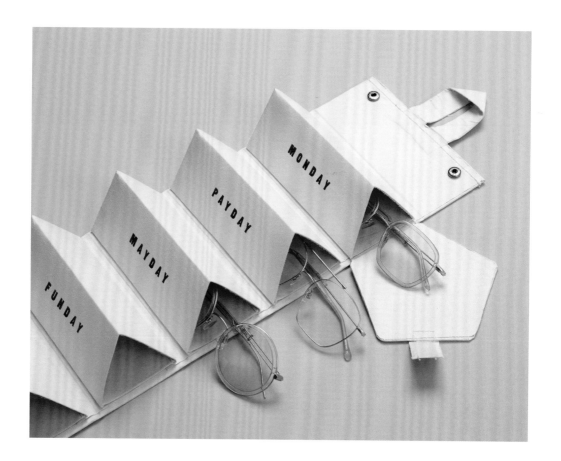

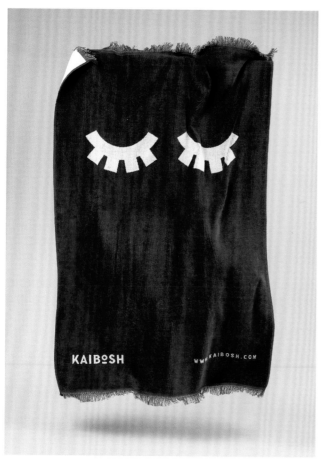

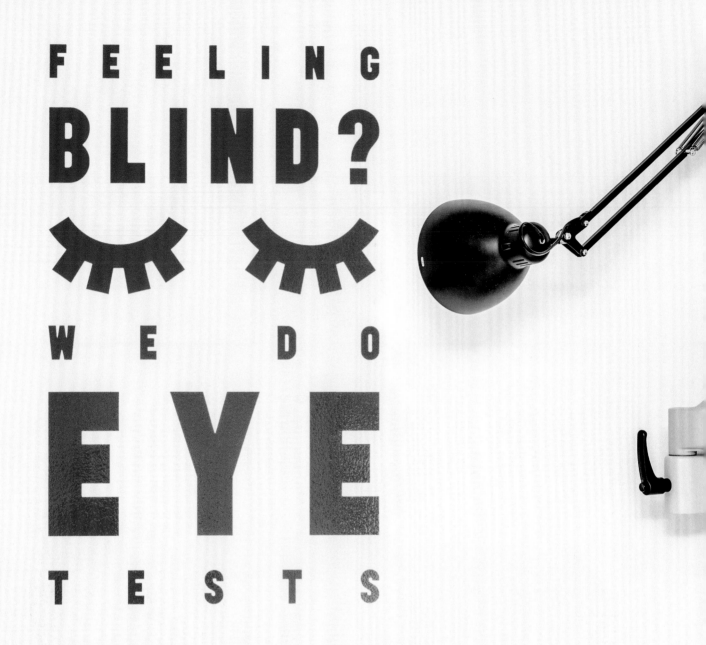

FEELING BLIND? WE DO EYE TESTS

"Some might say that Scandinavian design is minimalistic. But in the year of 2018 when we have been inspired by everything that a global internet offers, this idea is somewhat wrong since there are so many styles that provide inspiration. Scandinavian design is somehow undefinable."

WERKLIG

Werklig is a strategic brand design agency based in Helsinki, Finland. They design, sharpen, and evolve brands. They build brand strategies, design visual identities, and create solutions that boost sales, increase brand value, and build sustainable customer relationships. Their mission is to help their clients to conquer the world.

01. EMMA: In Search of the Present

"In Search of the Present" is a new visual layer to the existing black-and-white identity of EMMA Museum. The exhibition's identity is based on the continuous, chronic scrolling movement that people do when using their computers, phones and other devices. The movement can be seen in all of the applications of the identity, either as a cut-out text or physical movement.

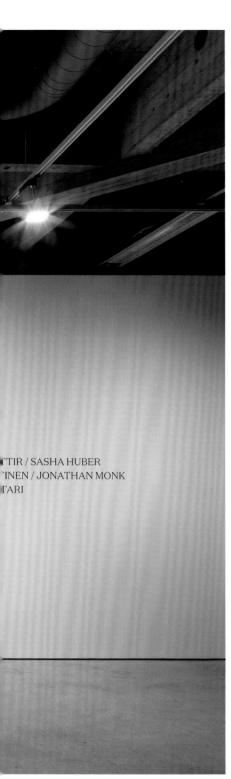

TIR / SASHA HUBER

INEN / JONATHAN MONK

TARI

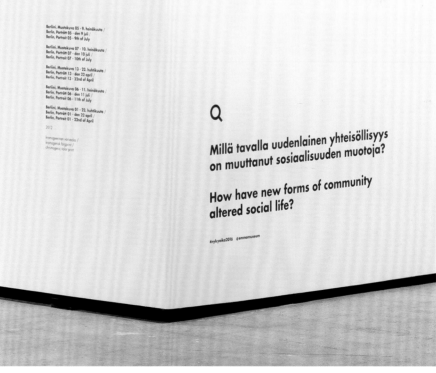

Q

Millä tavalla uudenlainen yhteisöllisyys
on muuttanut sosiaalisuuden muotoja?

How have new forms of community
altered social life?

#nykyaika2016 @emmamuseum

02. Suomen Jäätelö

Werklig created a brand identity for Suomen Jäätelö to communicate the super premium quality of its ice creams. The agency's work includes naming, packaging, web design, point-of-sale materials, and marketing communications. They chose an unconventionally shaped ice cream tub and combined the logo with a strong pattern, which was inspired by the perfect balance of elasticity and viscosity of a premium ice cream.

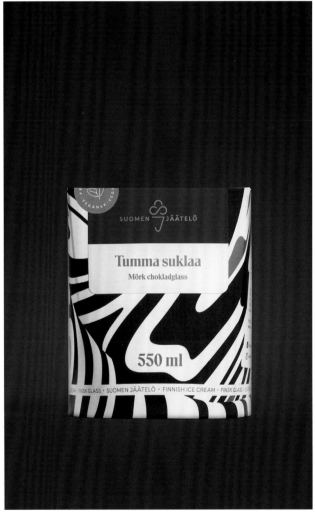

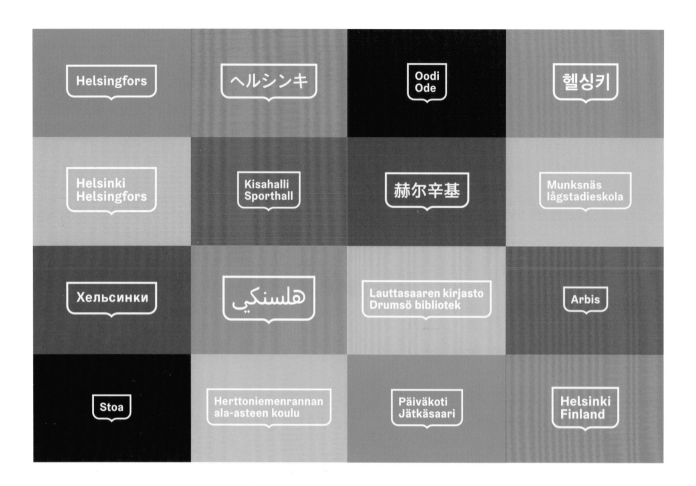

03. City of Helsinki

The rebranding of Helsinki respects the past and is both modern and timeless. The logo was based on the traditional Helsinki crest and made to adapt to any content, such as different languages. The brand's colors are subconsciously familiar to citizens—they are the colors used in the Helsinki crest, the cupola of Helsinki Cathedral, the tram and metro, etc. Werklig employed a custom typeface with typographic "wavy" details, Helsinki Grotesk by Camelot, to be used consistently in all Helsinki city communications.

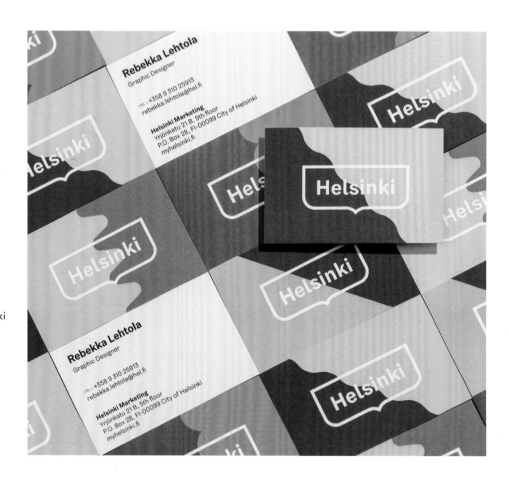

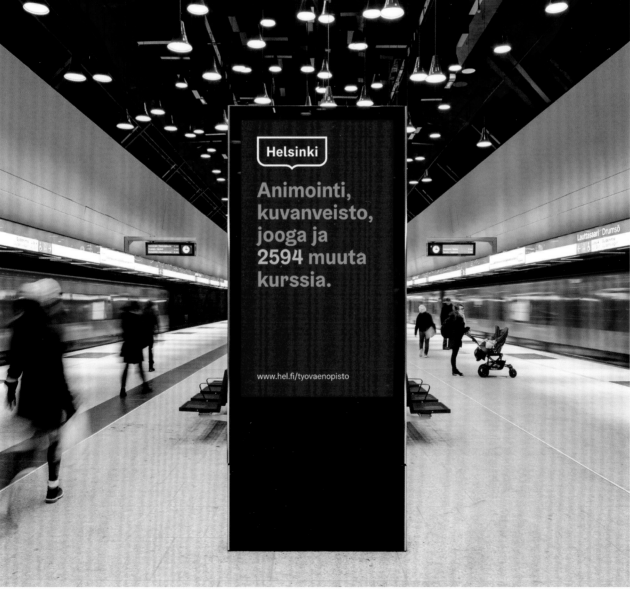

04. Holvi

Holvi is an intuitive professional banking tool for entrepreneurs and micro businesses. The logo is in the shape of a nonagon which rests firmly on its horizontal base to depict stability and reliability. The corners are slightly rounded to match the friendly brand tonality.

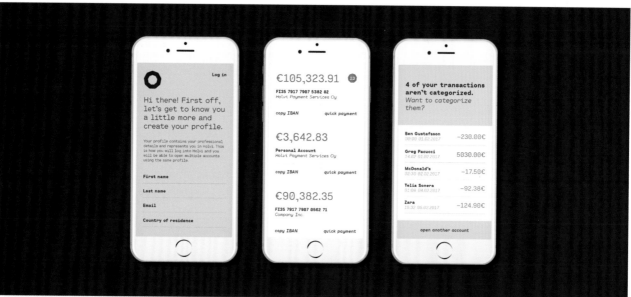

05. Helsinki City Museum

The Helsinki City Museum is the museum of Helsinki. Old everyday print materials from the museum's collections were used as the basis for its renewed visual narrative and then further transformed into a set of custom typefaces and colors. The design system functions as an authentic connection to Helsinki.

"It is vital to understand the relationship between the Scandinavian way of life and Scandinavian aesthetics. Some may see Scandinavian design just as a visual style or gimmick but it is actually the outcome of how Scandinavian people live, think, and observe their environment, turned into a visual and tangible form."

BEDOW

It all started in 2002 when Perniclas Bedow lost his day job at an advertising agency. Trying to impress Stockholm's design agencies with a lousy portfolio was not the easiest task and the industry's neglect was the push he needed to start his own studio—Bedow. In 2011, the designer Anders Bollman joined Bedow, and now the two run the studio together. Their work has been recognized for its simple, thoughtful, practical design. The team consists of five designers and resides in Stockholm, Sweden.

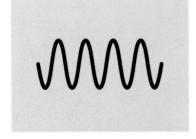

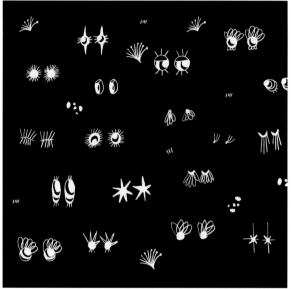

01. Fable Skateboards

Fable Skateboards is a new skate brand aimed at skaters who want to ride and make a difference at the same time. Half of Fable's profit goes to charity, mainly to projects that keep skateboarding an inclusive sport.

Fable Skateboards is an alternative to the established skate industry, aimed at skaters that want to ride and make a difference at the same time. Half of our profit, a clean 50-50 that is, goes to charity – mainly to projects that keep skateboarding an inclusive sport. Skate – and make a difference!

Follow us on instagram @fableskateboards!

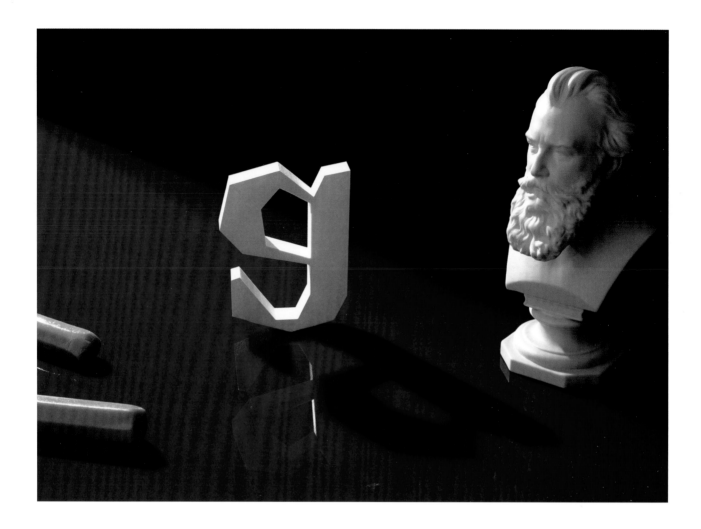

02. Gustav Almestål

This is the visual identity for Swedish photographer Gustav Almestål. A large component of his work focuses on the interaction between light and shadow. Bedow interpreted that interaction through a smart monogram: The shadow of the letter "g" looks like an "a."

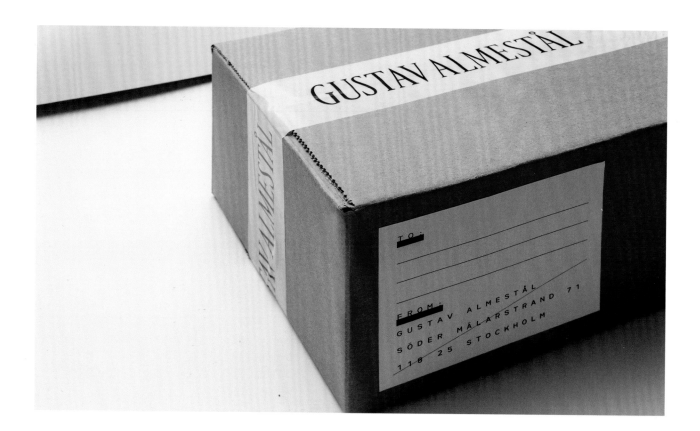

03. Helio

Helio is a co-working space based in Stockholm. Its visual
identity and communication concept are based on the spark
ignited by a collaboration of a group of people coming from
different fields.

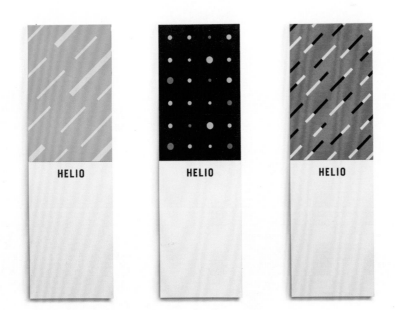

"Scandinavian design, for us, is a huge variety of beautiful work."

STUDIO AHREMARK

Studio Ahremark endeavors to provide clients with carefully crafted and conceptually appropriate design solutions. With a wide range of services, their goal is to help their clients build stronger and more durable brands with effective visual strategies that resonate well with audiences and generate positive business impacts.

01. Yx Visual Identity

Yx needed a concept that could illustrate durability and the trustworthiness of its products. The solution was to ground the visual identity in something almost archetypical. Inspired by Nordic nature and Scandinavian heritage, Studio Ahremark crafted an identity that would strongly emphasize the brand's dedication to traditional craft and materials.

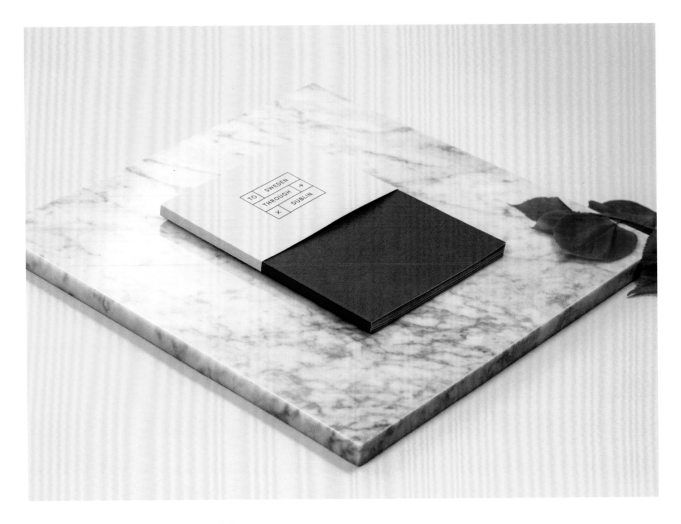

02. To Sweden through Dublin

This publication is a vivid and bright piece of design. Through the use of form, colors, typography, and texture, it becomes a design object, not merely something that provides insight and information.

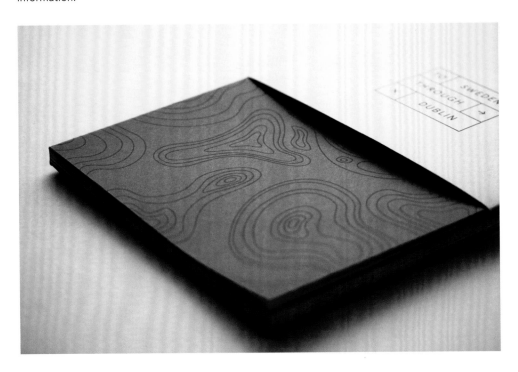

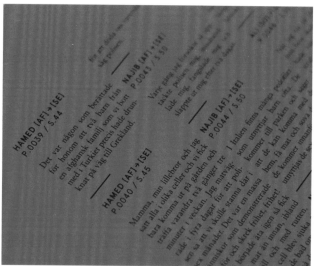

**Jag vill bara veta
om de lever.**

REZA / 16 / AFGHANISTAN

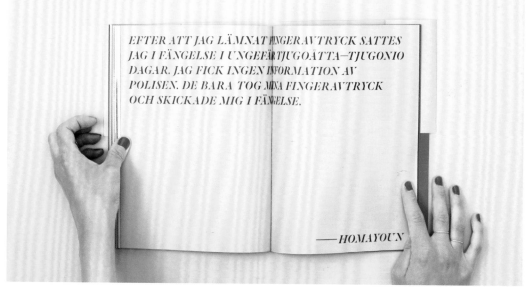

*EFTER ATT JAG LÄMNAT FINGERAVTRYCK SATTES
JAG I FÄNGELSE I UNGEFÄR TJUGOÅTTA–TJUGONIO
DAGAR. JAG FICK INGEN INFORMATION AV
POLISEN. DE BARA TOG MINA FINGERAVTRYCK
OCH SKICKADE MIG I FÄNGELSE.*

— HOMAYOUN

03. Saiy

Saiy, pronounced "Say," gives the devices in your home the ability to talk to one another. The design is a sophisticated visual system built on the concept of the tech community. The serif logo was constructed by using the shapes of a quotation mark to visualize the notion of "speech" and voice control.

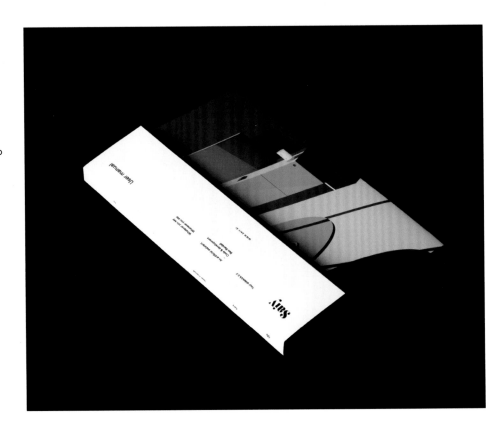

STUDIO AHREMARK

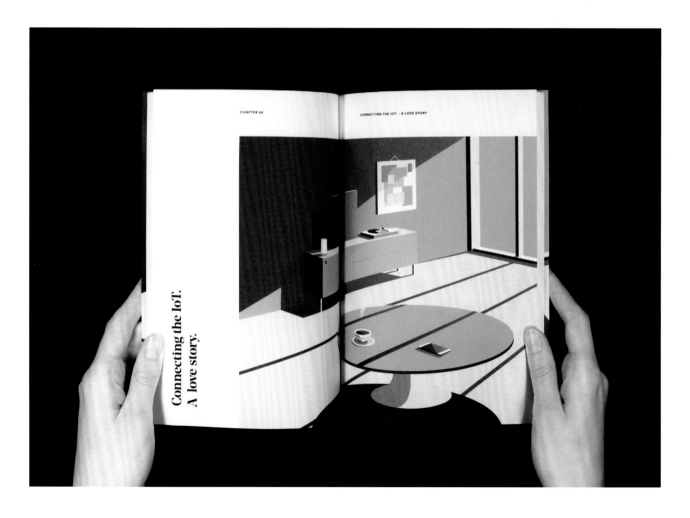

List of Devices

"Presently and historically, Scandinavian design is usually based around the ideas of simplicity and functionalism. Reduction and simplicity help in clarifying communicative aspects and minimize waste."

A seriously ⁰³· Connected home.

Saiy

INTRO—   COMMANDS   DEVELOPERS   ⋮⋮⋮

Need motivation: Just say 'coffee'

ALL COMMANDS   TAP TO LAUNCH SAIY

LARSSEN & AMARAL

Larssen & Amaral is a Norwegian design consultancy offering fully integrated design services. It gathers designers and creatives with diverse international backgrounds and has been working with branding, graphic design, and retail design for over fifteen years.

Larssen & Amaral

01. !Konferansen

!Konferansen is a new Norwegian conference for women, by women. The conferences aim to provoke change and inspire growth, setting focus on successful women and their stories. Each conference consists of a series of lectures, debates, and discussions. Larssen & Amaral was tasked with creating the new visual identity and marketing materials.

KONFERANSEN
BY KVINNERAADET

Konferansen som provoserer til endring
og inspirerer til vekst!

FOREDRAGSHOLDERE

JANOVE OTTESEN
SOLFRID FLATEBY
ZEKIYE NYLAND
BRIT LISE STEINKJELLÅ
HILDE LOREEN BENTSEN
NANCY HERZ

EDDA KINO, 3.NOVEMBER KL. 11-16

Finn ut mer om !Konferansen, og kjøp billett
til dag og kveldsarrangement på:

WWW.KONFERANSEN.NO

02. Formbar

Inspired by the glass-blowing process, Formbar's logo reflects the organic form and imperfections of glass. Since each hand-blown object is unique, Larssen & Amaral created an organic logo that allows for infinite variations.

LARSSEN & AMARAL

Formbar is a Norwegian glass studio producing handblown tableware, sophisticated glass design and art.

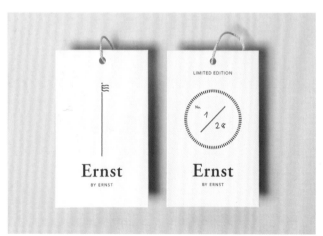

03. Ernst by Ernst

Ernst by Ernst is a new Norwegian menswear brand bringing elegance to everyday style. With a mission to bring a Scandinavian mentality to classic European tailoring, Ernst offers quality crafted menswear for the modern man. Larssen & Amaral was tasked with developing the complete brand and new e-commerce site.

Elegance for everyday style.
Welcome to the world of Ernst.

Ernst
BY ERNST

04. Qvalis

Larssen & Amaral created a visual identity that reflects the
balance and tension between fitness and wellbeing, presenting
Qvalis' holistic perspective on health: pairing exercise and
healthy eating with the reality of everyday life.

"Scandinavian design has traditionally been seen as a clean and minimalistic aesthetic, but over time a new spirit of adventure and experimentation has made its way into the visual language we use."

KOBRA
AGENCY

Kobra Agency partners with ambitious clients to develop strong and lasting brands. They offer a large range of services in the fields of brand strategy and design including naming, visual identity design, rebranding, creative and art direction, copywriting, and web design.

01. Starsquad

The new visual identity of Starsquad drew inspiration from the graphic of a running track and includes bold color. The symbol "SQ" taps into a long tradition of sports graphics and was designed as an homage to the classic 1968 Summer Olympics in Mexico City.

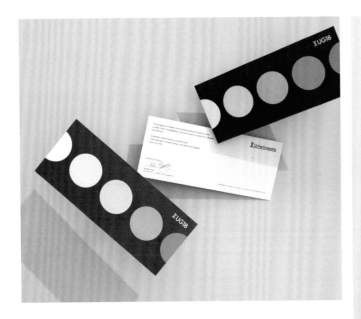

02. The Finnish Sports Gala

Kobra Agency created the new brand and visual identity for the Gala. Motion graphics created and implemented on TV, arena screens, and the gala stage, coupled with 3D mapping, bring the identity to life and elevate the brand experience to a new high.

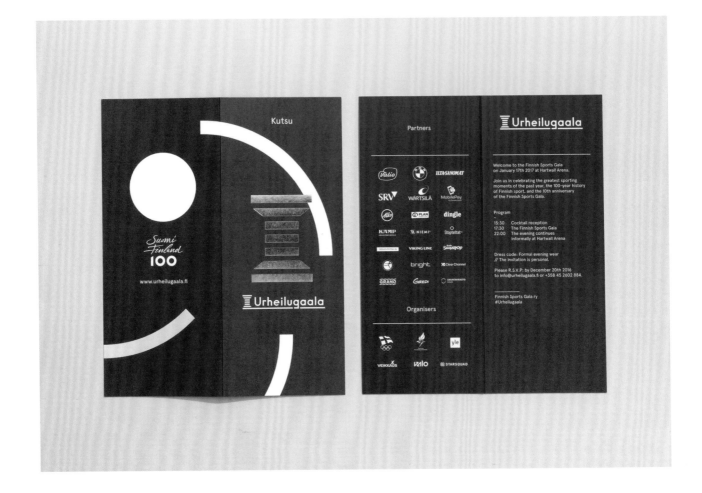

03. Förlaget

This is the visual identity for Förlaget, a Fenno-Swedish publishing house.

"We believe that a strong brand communicates a company's unique strengths and values by making the big ideas that drive the company accessible to its audience."

ACID AND MARBLE

Acid and Marble is a creative studio based in Stockholm, Sweden that delivers purpose- and concept-driven design and engaging experiences for businesses that want to stand out and step into the spotlight. Known for their conceptual focus, attention to detail, and use of typography, they immerse themselves in every project, creating consistent and engaging brand experiences. They believe that good design is a part of everyday life. It connects people with their emotions, gives them experiences, shapes their memories, and persuades them to act.

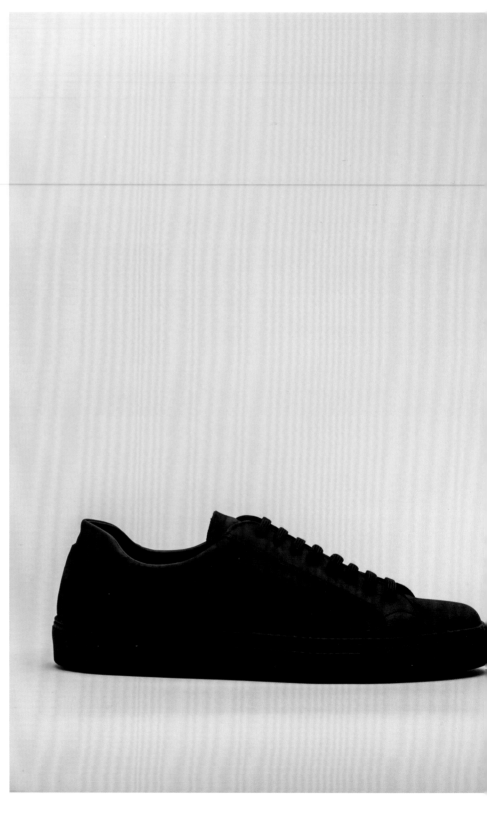

01. Sweyd Footwear

Acid and Marble created designs for Sweyed that blend Scandinavian design aesthetics with shoemaker heritage. They aimed to find the balance between both heritages, merging them into an identity that reflects the detailed craftsmanship of the shoes.

02. O–S–A

Acid and Marble developed a concept and interpretation of the track *Tiger* from the latest album *Wild Youth*, by Steve Angello in a collaboration with Odeur Studios. The work resulted in a pattern symbolizing a feeling that truly captures our journey in life, which sometimes leaves us with painful wounds like scratches from a tiger. This is what paved the way for O–S–A (Odeur–Steve–Angello), a unique capsule collection consisting of twelve signature garments. All styles are unisex and suitable for both adults and children.

ACID AND MARBLE

"Scandinavian design
is always functional,
sustainable and strives
to be long-lasting
and have a great care
for details. It is calm
but expressive and it
respects nature and
the beauty of it."

Track—TIGER
Album—WILD YOUTH
O—S—A

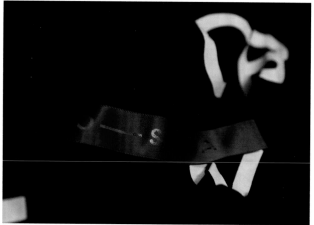

ACID AND MARBLE

HENRIK
NYGREN DESIGN

Henrik Nygren Design analyzes
the client's market potential
and comes up with a strategy
in accordance with this
potential. The agency works
on the design and production
of corporate identities, websites,
books, exhibitions, packaging,
magazines, and campaigns, etc.

Henrik Nygren—Design

01. Wästberg

Commissioned by the lighting company Wästberg, Henrik Nygren Design completed the invitation, *Wästberg Catalogue 2016*, printed matter, lamps, manifesto, tote bags, and an exhibition for the Stockholm Furniture & Light Fair in 2017.

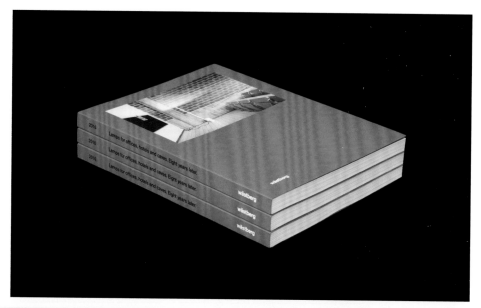

Form Us With Love, is the international design studio founded in 2005. Since its conception, the studio has burned with a passion for design and its democratic potential. Its belief is that we all have a right to meaningful design. At the studio's core lies a process that blends traditional creative practices (real prototyping over CAD) with a lean, strategic application. The central intention is to evolve with the needs of each project, its place in the market and the ever changing needs of real people.

Today, the work of Form Us With Love falls into three areas: Consultancy—an engagement in products, ranges, collaborations and spaces for clients around the world, Ventures—disciplined and holistic approaches, to launch and build brands, and Civic—based on knowledge transfers and sharing of experiences, actively contributing to the broader spectra of design.

02. FUWL

The exhibition "I–X" at the Royal Academy of Fine Arts was commissioned by the Stockholm-based design studio Form Us With Love to celebrate the company's ten-year-anniversary and for Stockholm Furniture & Light Fair in winter 2016.

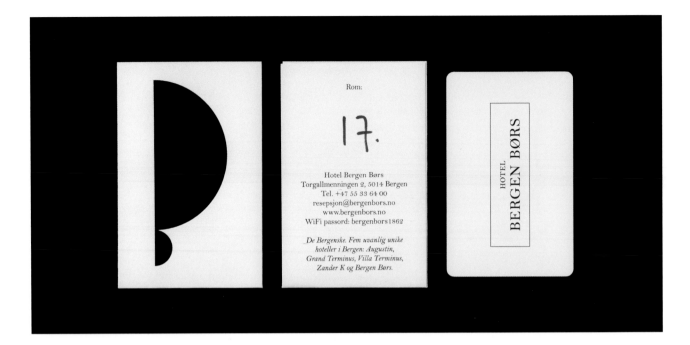

03. Hotel Bergen Børs

This is a new identity for Hotel Bergen Børs, a truly unique
hotel in Bergen. It was commissioned by the hotel company De
Bergenske, which also operates the hotels Villa Terminus, Grand
Hotel Terminus, Hotel Zander K, and Hotel Augustin.

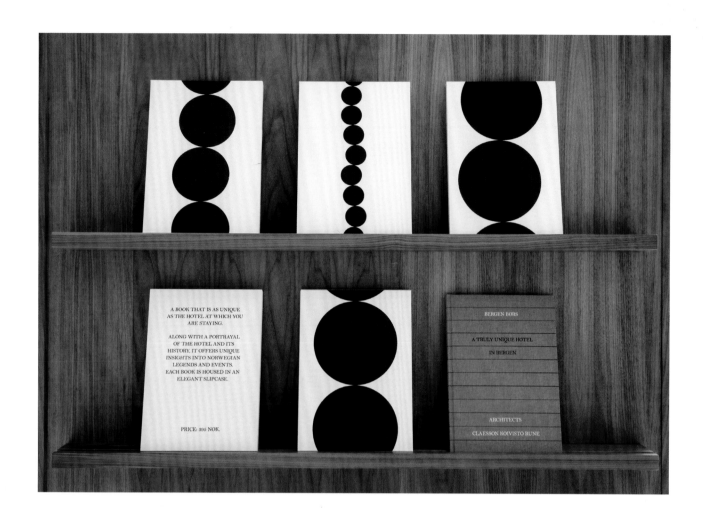

A BOOK THAT IS AS UNIQUE
AS THE HOTEL AT WHICH YOU
ARE STAYING.

ALONG WITH A PORTRAYAL
OF THE HOTEL AND ITS
HISTORY, IT OFFERS UNIQUE
INSIGHTS INTO NORWEGIAN
LEGENDS AND EVENTS.
EACH BOOK IS HOUSED IN AN
ELEGANT SLIPCASE.

PRICE: 395 NOK.

BERGEN BØRS

A TRULY UNIQUE HOTEL

IN BERGEN

ARCHITECTS

CLAESSON KOIVISTO RUNE

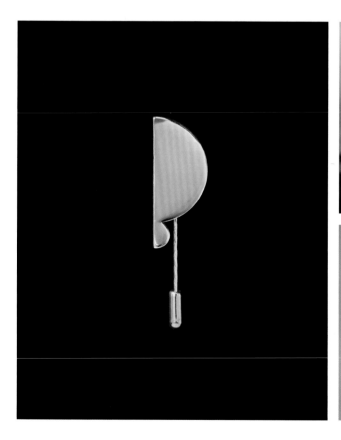

DE
BERGENSKE

"We mainly deal with analyzing the client's market potential, with strategy in accordance with this potential."

HENRIK NYGREN DESIGN

HENRIK NYGREN DESIGN

KURPPA HOSK

Founded in 2009, Kurppa Hosk is a fast-moving and human-centered design agency. They collaborate with forward-looking businesses and brands that are in the process of change. Kurppa Hosk helps them to facilitate this change by defining and designing purpose-driven experiences that strengthen the relationships with users, customers, employees, and society at large.

01. REF

Kurppa Hosk created a brand identity comprised of simple elements: a sophisticated wordmark, slim typography, and modest, earthy color palettes. The colors were the foundation for the packaging system, making it easy to navigate through different product categories and individual products on offer. Kurppa Hosk also designed REF's new website and collateral materials, giving the brand a recognizable and consistent feel at every point.

KURPPA HOSK

02. Designtorget

The guiding star for the brand identity was Designtorget's Scandinavian legacy of simplicity and clarity. The "D" and the "T" of the logo form a symbol that can be interpreted as two objects or a friendly character. The renewed brand identity is a result of systematic typography and a set of sophisticated colors.

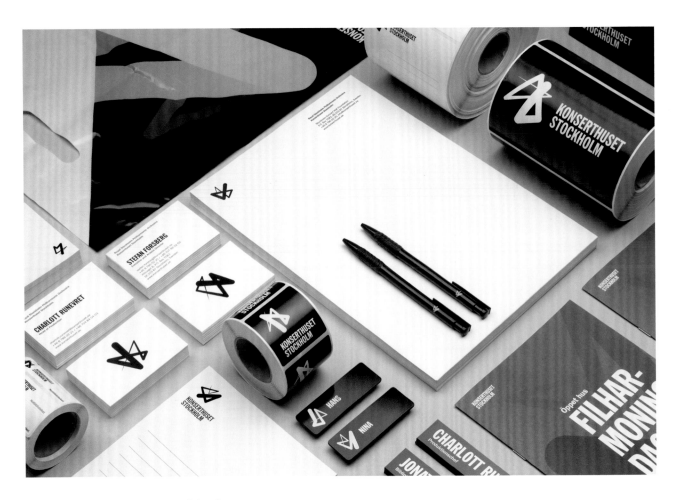

03. Konserthuset Stockholm

This visual identity includes an ever-changing organic symbol that represents and unites both Konserthuset Stockholm and the Royal Stockholm Philharmonic Orchestra. It also serves as a "musical signature" that conveys the movement and energy of the music.

"We call our methodology
business artistry. It intertwines
business thinking and insight
with imagination, intuition,
iteration, beauty, and meticulous
craftsmanship."

JENS NILSSON

Jens Nilsson is a Stockholm-based, award-winning graphic designer and art director with over ten years of industry experience. He is also the former art director at the famed design agency Snask.

01. PangPang Can Release

Jens did the beer label design and art direction for PangPang Brewery's Can Release. The graphic elements in black and white were screen-printed on a silver-foiled die-cut label.

02. Maldini Studios

The identity of Maldini Studios has a high focus on textures and materials with the custom-made typeface, Donadoni, as the main component. The letterpress-printed stationery is printed on various textured papers from GF Smith and Arjowiggins.

JENS NILSSON

"Whether modern or not modern,
I guess Scandinavian design stands
for simplicity and minimalism."

JENS NILSSON

25AH

25AH is a Stockholm-based multidisciplinary brand and design agency that offers a commercial strategy for creative and unconventional design and identity solutions.

01. Stromma Arkipelag

Strömma Arkipelag reflects a modern lifestyle on the archipelago. With moody watercolor drawings and photography, the visual design creates a harmonious yet dynamic feel, echoing the location of this residential property development project.

02. Gretas

Gretas is a café located at the Hotel Haymarket by Scandic in Stockholm. The identity is based on an illustration created by 25AH. Different sections of the illustration are used as patterns, extending throughout the identity. The project was developed in collaboration with architects at koncept TM.

03. Caldo Coffee

Caldo Coffee is a café located in Scandic Continental. 25AH created the whole identity including logotype, signage, and take-away packages. Neon signs and custom-built menu boards with changeable letters were used to create an urban feel, reflecting the café's central location. The project was developed in collaboration with architects at koncept TM.

04. Time Building

Time Building is a conference and office center located in Sweden's Silicon Valley, Kista. Based on a design concept inspired by New York City and its high space, the offices are numbered and displayed like a digital clock, with floor numbers to the left and room numbers to the right. The project was developed in collaboration with architects at koncept TM.

05. Grand Central by Scandic

This hotel is located in Stockholm's old printing district and is one of the few buildings that survived after the area's modernization. 25AH drew inspiration from the past of this region and created an identity centered on news printing typography. The project was developed in collaboration with architects at koncept TM.

"We believe in connecting people emotionally with a brand."

KASPER PYNDT

Kasper Pyndt is a type and graphic designer living in Copenhagen and The Hague. The starting point and main engine of his practice is his passion for type, language, and the relationship between the two. Through this practice, he aims to develop straightforward and unpretentious design solutions that are conceptually sturdy, contextually self-aware, and personally challenging. Kasper creates books, posters, typefaces, visual identities, and websites. He is always open to new types of collaborations and commissions.

Kasper Pyndt

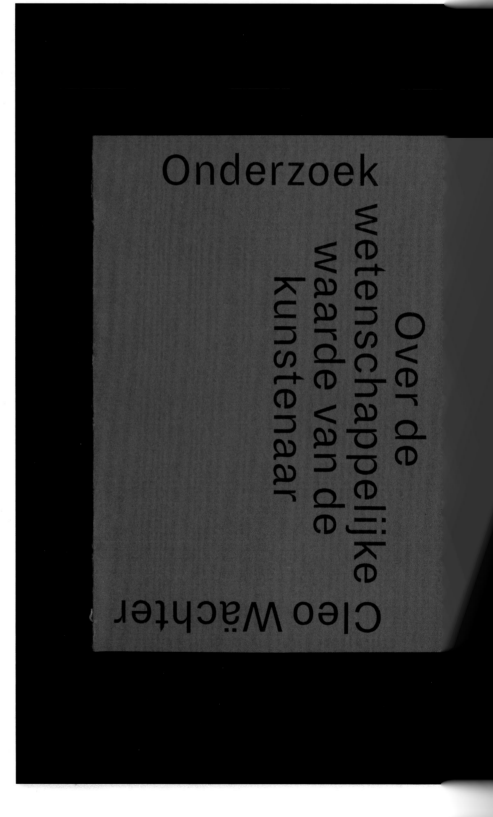

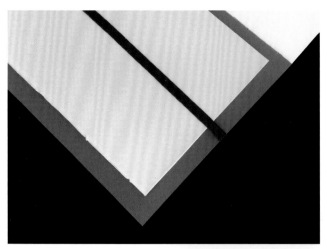

01. Onderzoek

The correlation of art and scientific research is the focal point of Cleo Wächter's thesis. In designing the book, Kasper Pyndt wanted readers to feel as if they are taking part in the research. Every chapter ends with a text-box in which the reader can contribute by adding personal annotations. A small selection of the author's photos is hidden within the blue chapter pages, adding a sense of research and discovery to the reading experience.

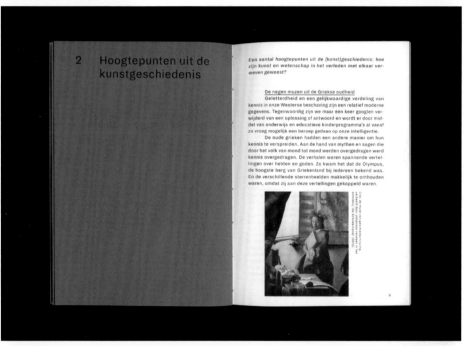

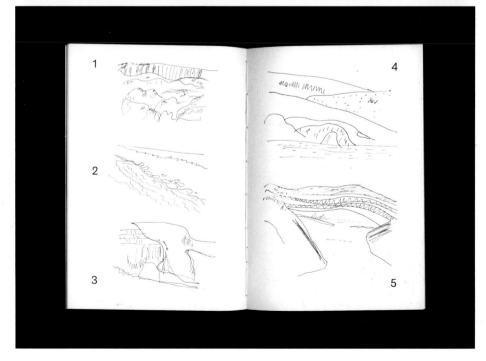

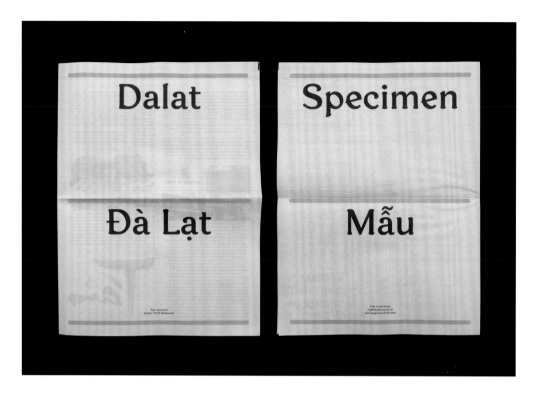

02. Dalat Specimen

This project is a newsprint specimen for the typeface Dalat.
The specimen includes an essay by Yours Truly on Vietnamese
graphic design.

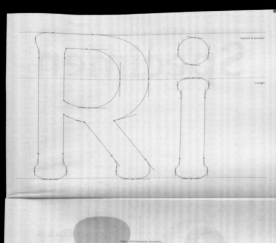

ABCDEFGHIJKLMNOPQRSTUVWXYZ
abcdefghijklmnopqrstuvwxyz

ÀÁÂÃÄĀĂĄÅÅÁÀÂÂĀĀÆĆČÇĊĎĐĐĔĒĖĖ
ÈĒÊĖÈĔÊĖÊĒĖĖĘĠĢĦÍÌÎÏĬĬĪĮİĶĹĽĻŁŃŇÑŅ
ÓÔÒÕÖŌŎŐŒÓÖÔÒÕŎŐÕÖØŘŖ
ŚŞŠŢŤŢŢÚÙÛÜŮŪŪŲŮÚŮÜÛÚŮ
ŴŴŴÝŶŸÝÝỲŹŽŻ
àáâãāăǎåāạãâāæćčçċðďđèêêẽęéééèêë
èḙêĕğġhịṇĳḳĺŀ·łńņŷńǒ́ộǎ́ồṓ̀ǒ̀ồộ̀

"Cooper Black is extremely used, together with a few more fonts."

Hồ Chí Minh	1880–1969
Tôn Đức Thắng	1888–1980
Trường Chinh	1907–1988
Võ Chí Công	1912–2011

Mọi người đều có quyền tự do tham gia vào đời sống văn hoá của cộng đồng, được thưởng thức nghệ thuật và chia xẻ những thành tựu và lợi ích của tiến bộ khoa học. Mọi người đều có quyền được bảo hộ đối với những quyền lợi về vật chất và tinh thần xuất phát từ công trình khoa học, văn học và nghệ thuật mà người đó là tác giả.

Everyone has the right freely to participate in the cultural life of the community, to enjoy the arts and to share in the scientific advancement and its benefits. Everyone has the right to the protection of the moral and material interests resulting from any scientific, literary or artistic production of which he is the author.

Obstacles & Prospects

A. de Rhodes

Crossbreed
Crossbreed
Crossbreed
Crossbreed
Crossbreed
Crossbreed
Crossbreed
Crossbreed
Crossbreed
Crossbreed
Crossbreed
Crossbreed
Crossbreed
Crossbreed

"A lot of those who are trained in Western countries, are working hard to define our visual cultures"

03. Do We Need Masters?

Kasper Pyndt utilized a number of Hans Wegner's chairs to form an alphabet, removing their original function and redefining their usage. The goal was to challenge the authority of Wegner's work and cheekily ask the question: Do we need masters?

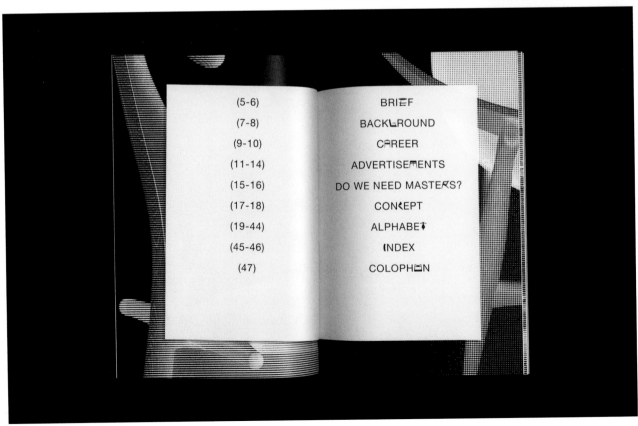

BACKGROUND

Hans Wegner, who had an education in carpentry, designed more than 500 chairs during his carreer. Most notably, China Chair (1944), Peacock Chair (1947), Y-Chair (1950), Valet Chair (1953) and The Round Chair (1949), the last of which were famously utilized in the television debate between John F. Kennedy and Richard Nixon.

During his carreer Wegner received a number of awards, among those The 8th International Design Award (Osaka) and Lunningprisen. Despite prestigious awards and a high regard, Wegner was a modest and socially engaged person, that did not demand a lot of attention.

His style, that came out of the Moder-nist tradition, has been described as Organic Functionality, which refers to the rationalism and minimalism in his designs along with a dedication to exposing/mixing materials and working fluently with shape. Decoration is non-existing in his work.

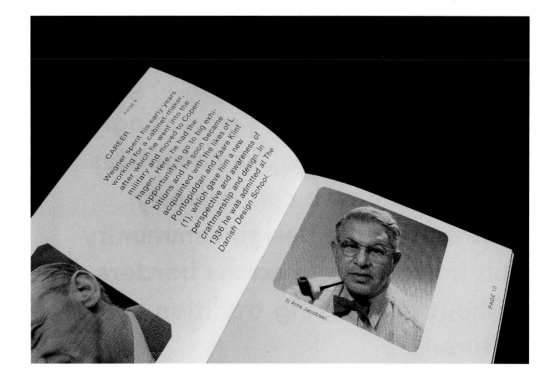

CAREER

Wegner spent his early years working for a cabinet-maker, after which he went into the military and moved to Copenhagen. Here, he had the opportunity to go to big exhibitions and he soon became acquainted with the likes of L. Pontopiddan and Kaare Klint (1), which gave him a new perspective and awareness of craftmanship and design. In 1936 he was admitted at The Danish Design School.

PAGE 9

2) Arne Jacobsen

PAGE 10

Ad for the AP chair, stressing
the craftmanship behind it.

he tradition for Scandinavian
nimalism is still highly influential
product and furniture design—
pecially in Denmark—but in graphic
sign, it is becoming increasingly
ficult to tell European countries
art, as the web continuously
ntributes to a design community
at borrows from across borders
thout considering tradition or
lture."

KASPER PYNDT

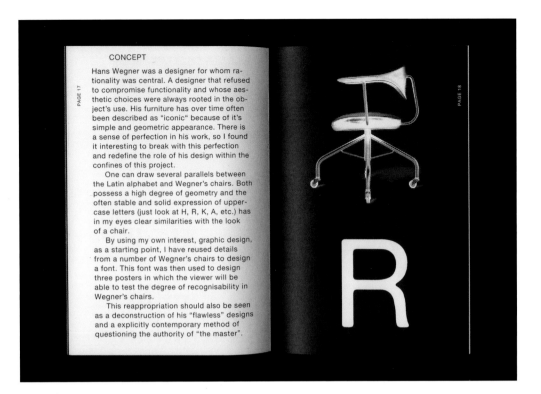

CONCEPT

Hans Wegner was a designer for whom rationality was central. A designer that refused to compromise functionality and whose aesthetic choices were always rooted in the object's use. His furniture has over time often been described as "iconic" because of it's simple and geometric appearance. There is a sense of perfection in his work, so I found it interesting to break with this perfection and redefine the role of his design within the confines of this project.

One can draw several parallels between the Latin alphabet and Wegner's chairs. Both possess a high degree of geometry and the often stable and solid expression of upper-case letters (just look at H, R, K, A, etc.) has in my eyes clear similarities with the look of a chair.

By using my own interest, graphic design, as a starting point, I have reused details from a number of Wegner's chairs to design a font. This font was then used to design three posters in which the viewer will be able to test the degree of recognisability in Wegner's chairs.

This reappropriation should also be seen as a deconstruction of his "flawless" designs and a explicitly contemporary method of questioning the authority of "the master".

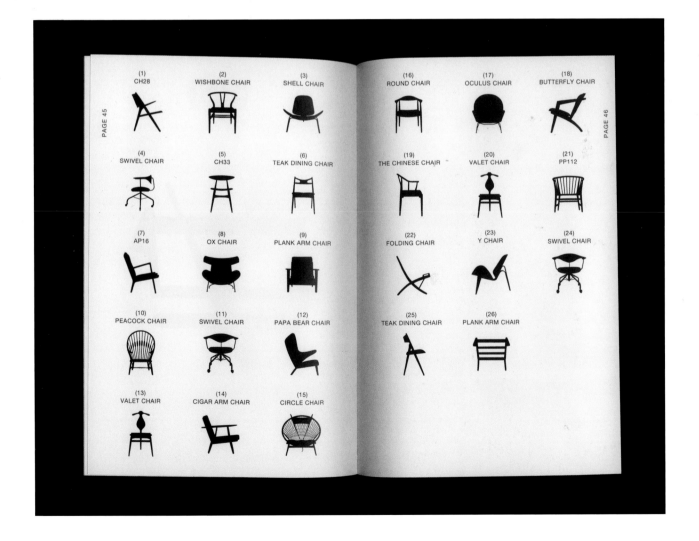

(1) CH28

(2) WISHBONE CHAIR

(3) SHELL CHAIR

(4) SWIVEL CHAIR

(5) CH33

(6) TEAK DINING CHAIR

(7) AP16

(8) OX CHAIR

(9) PLANK ARM CHAIR

(10) PEACOCK CHAIR

(11) SWIVEL CHAIR

(12) PAPA BEAR CHAIR

(13) VALET CHAIR

(14) CIGAR ARM CHAIR

(15) CIRCLE CHAIR

(16) ROUND CHAIR

(17) OCULUS CHAIR

(18) BUTTERFLY CHAIR

(19) THE CHINESE CHAIR

(20) VALET CHAIR

(21) PP112

(22) FOLDING CHAIR

(23) Y CHAIR

(24) SWIVEL CHAIR

(25) TEAK DINING CHAIR

(26) PLANK ARM CHAIR

NICKLAS HASLESTAD

NORWAY

- Graphic Design
- Branding
- Print Design

Nicklas Haslestad is a Norwegian designer who graduated from Westerdals ACT. He works with clients worldwide including MasterCard, Adidas, Nike, Oslo Lufthavn, Westerdals, etc.

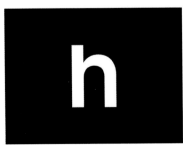

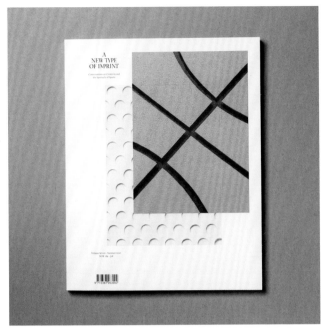

01. A New Type of Imprint II

Nicklas did the design for *A New Type of Imprint: Conversations on Creativity and the Spectacle of Sports*, Chapter 2. The layout and design were exclusively inspired by common denominators in sports.

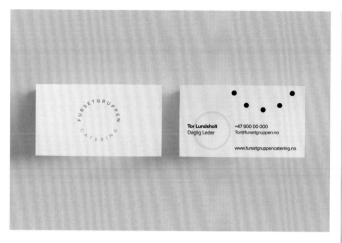

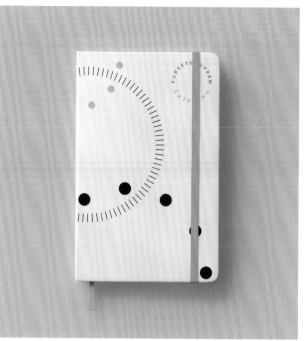

02. Fursetgruppen Catering

The concept of this identity was carved down to the bone with the single keyword "plate." This geometric form gave Nicklas the idea to create a universe of abstract circles to emphasize the different characteristics of Fursetgruppen Catering.

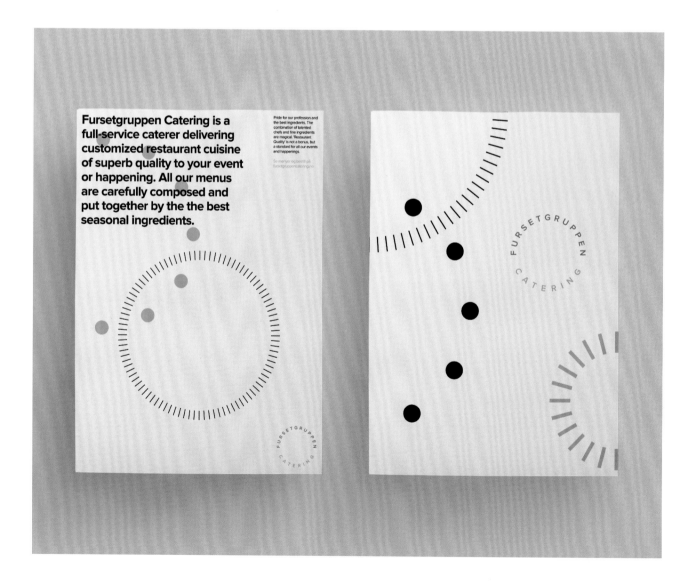

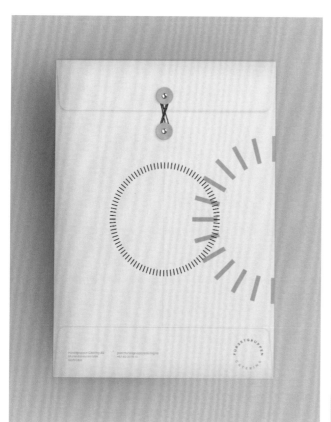

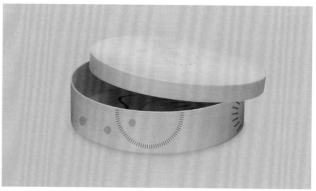

03. Dualog

This identity concept explores and visualizes the idea of dialogue and duality in the phrase "Ship to shore." The identity is anchored with visual references to the Arctic Circle, which influenced a custom logotype and logo where the central concepts are visualized as an image of the horizon.

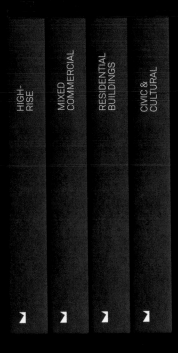

04. Mike Kelley

Mike Kelley is a Los Angeles-based photographer specializing in architectural photos. The visual identity for his website has a basis in the Fibonacci sequence, relevant for both architecture and photography. With a bold yet minimalistic and direct approach, the identity highlights and displays Mike Kelley's beautiful photography.

05. mbraced.by

The logo of mbraced.by, a brand of men's accessories, is based on circles, a reference to the product. The packaging system includes three carefully selected high-quality materials and the lid is crafted with matte, canvas-structured paper to communicate the concept of nature.

NICKLAS HASLESTAD

06. BA_53

Inspired by the location of this Oslo restaurant, Nicklas created an identity that is rooted in the area's history yet speaks for a young generation of ambitious chefs. The menu of BA_53 changes in pace with the Nordic seasons and the color scheme changes accordingly. Photos by Marte Garmann.

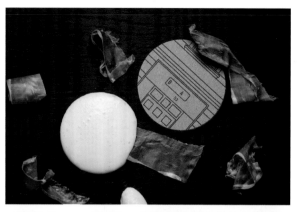

"Scandinavian design is anchored in simplicity, purity, and elegance, in our opinion. It is design built on a strong, timeless concept, executed with only relevant elements."

NICKLAS HASLESTAD

STOCKHOLM
DESIGN LAB

Stockholm Design Lab (SDL) transforms brands and businesses with simple, remarkable ideas. They think at a global level and work across continents. And they keep an unswerving focus on what lasts. They embrace the values: on clients rather than projects; on truth rather than triviality; on intelligence rather than speculation; and on design that endures and makes a difference.

SDL™

poc

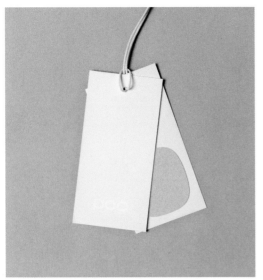

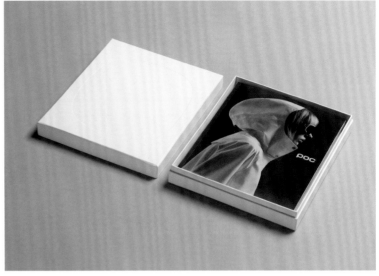

01. Poc and Forth

Taking a leap towards a more sophisticated look, yet staying true to its existing aesthetics, Stockholm Design Lab created a visual identity for Poc 2005. They developed a toolkit for the release of the new "Poc and Forth" collection which includes art direction, the design of images, brochures, hangtags with reflective, detachable stickers, and the work/look-book, which comes encased in a limited-edition handmade box.

02. Bonniers Konsthall

This identity is built on dialogue and communication and aims to enhance the visitor's experience. Typography became an important carrier of the identity as SDL sought a flexible system that could carry many different expressions, depending on the exhibition or event. The interior design was done by Marge Architects.

30 ÅR MED M R
BONNIER DA
STIFTELSE

PER HITTNER
STEF KARLSSON

BONN
KONS

BJÖRN PERBORG
CHARLOTTE ENST
PETRA LINDHOLM
SONJA NILSSON
STINA STIGELL
THOMAS BROOM
ANN BÖTTCHER
GUNNEL WAHLSTR
TILDA LOVELL
LISA JEANNIN
LISA JONASSON
JOHAN SVENSSON
LINA SELANDER
LARS BRUNSTRÖM
NINIA SVERDRUP
CAROLINE MÅRTENSS
JOHANNES HELDÉN
MARTIN SUNDVALL
EVAMARIE LINDAHL
JESSICA FAISS
MATHIAS KRISTERSSON
KRISTINA MATOUSCH
SOFIA BÄCKLUND
VIKTOR ROSDAHL

PAUL FÄGERSKIÖLD
JENNY YURSHANSK
KICO WIGREN
OLOF LINDSTRÖM
NADJA BOURNONVIL
PAULIINA PIETILÄ
SARA WALLGREN
JOSEF BULL
NANNA NORDSTRÖM
OLOF INGER
DIT-CILINN
ELLISIF HALS
GIDEONSSON / LON
LINUS NORDENSSON NGBERG

28 AUG

BJÖRN FRÖBERG
CHARLOTTE ENSTRÖM
PETRA LINDHOLM
SONJA NILSSON
STINA STIGELL
THOMAS BROOMÉ
ANN BÖTTCHER
GUNNEL WÅHLSTRAND
TILDA LOVELL

MARTIN ÅLUND
NYC, 1994

Olja på pannå / Oil on panel. 36 x 50 cm.

Stipendiat / Grant recipient 1989

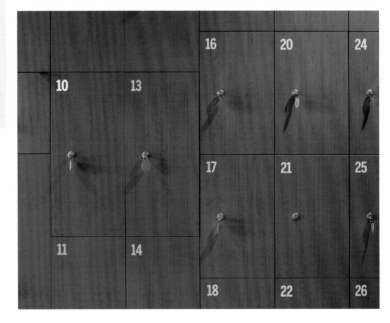

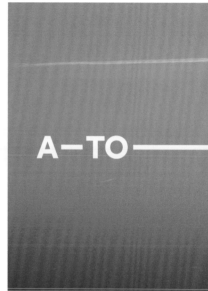

03. A–TO–B

Venue Retail Group approached SDL with a request: They wanted to create something new and refreshing in the bag retail market. They wanted a place that gathers and provides great, smart, and helpful products for people on the move. With this vision in mind, SDL created A–TO–B, a modern, mobile, and flexible brand with a clear purpose: to be there when you move from point A to point B, and every step in between.

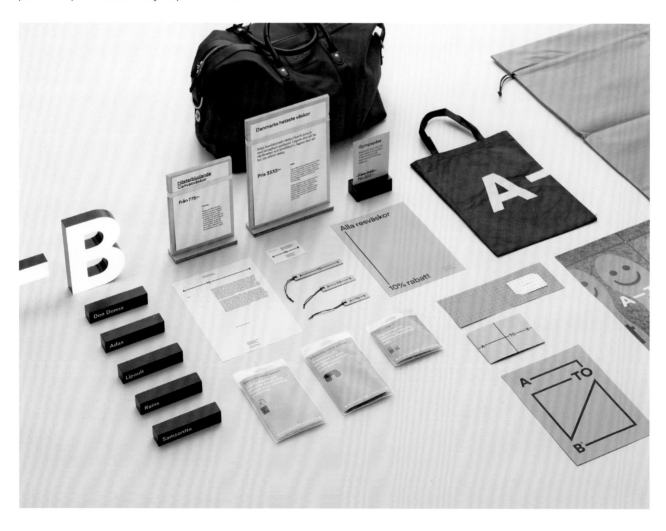

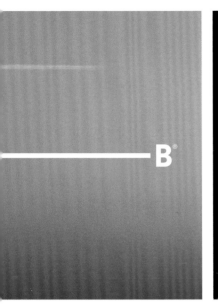

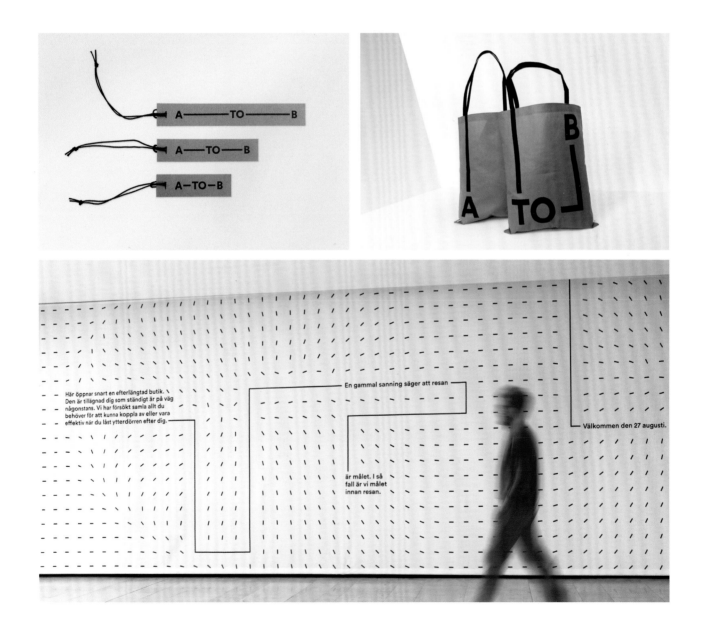

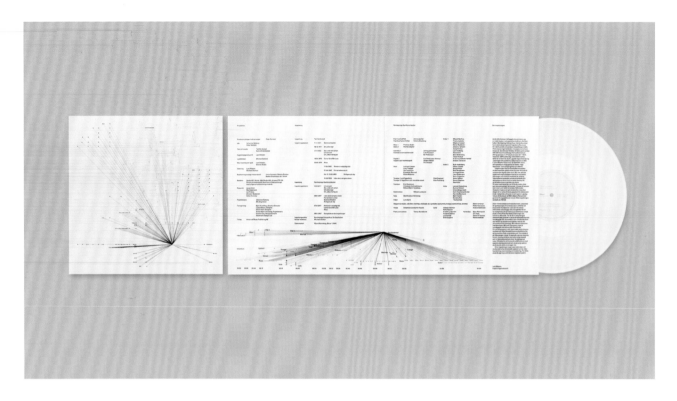

04. The Remastering of Ted Gärdestad

This visual identity not only symbolizes the music's note sheet, movement, and flow but also represents collaboration. The system is highly recognizable yet flexible, as each song has its own unique composition. Black is used for singles and white for the album. In motion graphics, the elements embody scenes drawn from the lyrics that flow with the music and follow its dynamics.

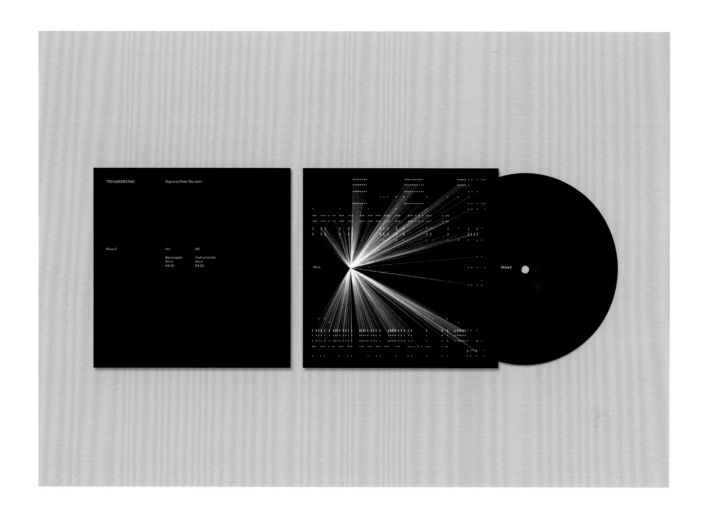

05. Moderna Museet

Moderna Museet, Sweden's national museum of contemporary art, opened on Skeppsholmen, Stockholm in 1958. SDL took inspiration from the *1983 25th Anniversary Catalog* designed by Robert Rauschenberg. Rauschenberg's "Moderna Museet" signature was arresting, compelling, and expressive, putting the museum back on the modern art map. The system of unstuffy, airport-style backlit signs that SDL designed, with the special version of Wim Crouwel's Gridnik typeface, continues to guide visitors around the museum building. This project was completed in collaboration with Greger Ulf Nilson, Henrik Nygren, Rafael Moneo, Marge Architects (MM Stockholm), and Tham Videgård (MM Malmö).

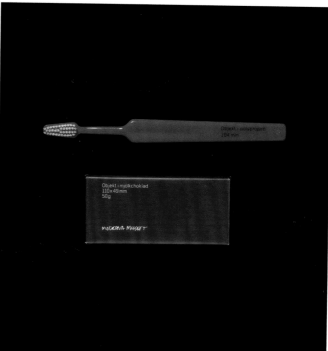

"Scandinavian design is about simplicity and clarity. But not always."

KUUDES

Kuudes is a Nordic insight, strategy, and design agency with offices in Helsinki and Stockholm. The agency combines in-depth consumer insights, products, service innovations, branding, and multi-disciplinary designs to create strong brands that people love.

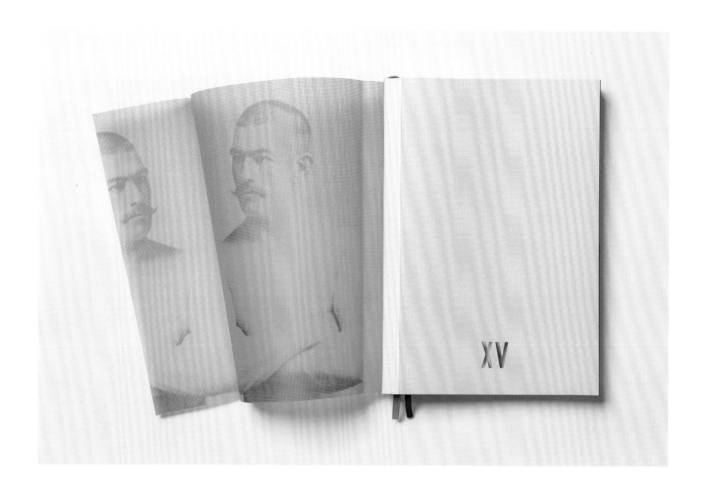

01. Vuoden Huiput XV

Vuoden Huiput is Finland's most significant annual creative design competition. Kuudes created for them a striking identity that celebrates the championship in a witty and playful manner.

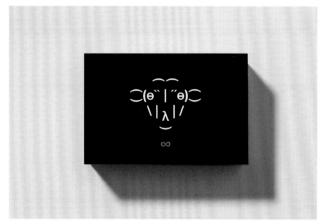

02. 8-bit-sheep

This visual identity for a digital strategy network is made entirely with Helvetica characters. The fittingly-named lambda, 11th letter of the Greek alphabet, is positioned as the nose. The number 8 reoccurs in the lamb's eyes as the symbol theta, coincidentally the 8th letter in the Greek alphabet.

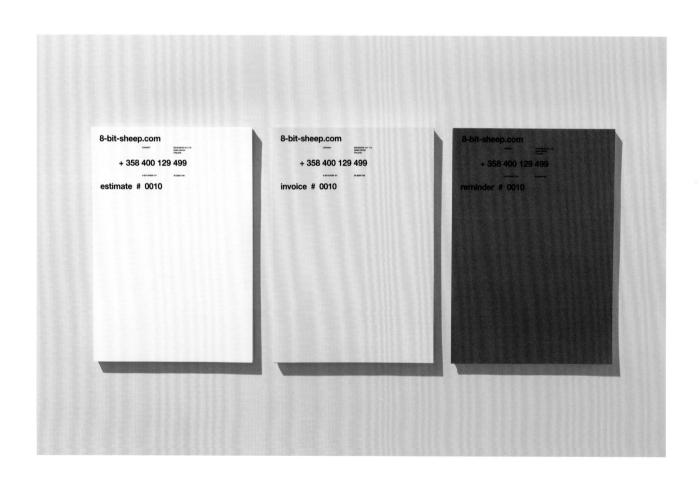

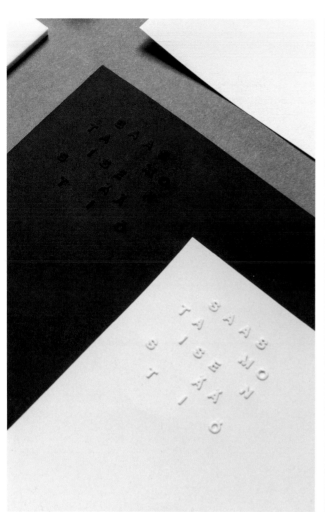

03. Saastamoinen Foundation

Kuudes designed for this cherished culture brand an identity that supports their contemporary, international, and leadership position. The letters in the logo are not fixed—they can form abstract combinations. This approach has led to a variety of stunning printed materials and animations.

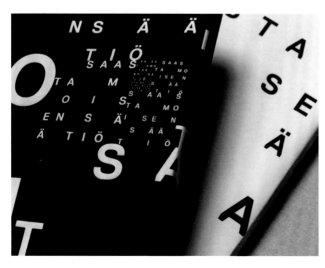

04. Alko Töölöntorii

To celebrate Alko's 85th anniversary, Kuudes created a one-of-a-kind liquor store in the spirit of the 1930s. The nostalgic retail design takes customer service to another level.

"The modern Scandinavian design values authenticity and social relevance—believing in your own thing and making a change for the better."

INDEX

25AH

www.25ah.se

P174–185

ACID AND MARBLE

acidandmarble.com

P144–149

BEDOW

BLEED

BOND CREATIVE AGENCY

HENRIK NYGREN DESIGN

Henrik Nygren—Design

JENS NILSSON

KASPER PYNDT

Kasper Pyndt

KOBRA AGENCY

KOBRA

KURPPA HOSK

KUUDES

6.

LARSSEN & AMARAL

Larssen & Amaral

LUNDGREN+LINDQVIST

NICKLAS HASLESTAD

OEDIPE

OLSSØNBARBIERI

SNASK

snask.com

P086–095

snask

STOCKHOLM DESIGN LAB

www.stockholmdesignlab.se

P208–221

SDL™

STUDIO AHREMARK

www.studioahremark.com

P118–125

WERKLIG

www.werklig.com

P096–109

WERKLIG

ACKNOWLEDGEMENTS

We would like to express our gratitude to all of the designers and companies for their generous contribution of images, ideas, and concepts. We are also very grateful to many other people whose names do not appear in the credits but who made specific contributions and provided support. Without them, the successful compilation of this book would not be possible. Special thanks to all of the contributors for sharing their innovation and creativity with all of our readers around the world.